HARVEST US HOME

Other works by Rachel Callahan, C.S.C.,
and Rea McDonnell, S.S.N.D.,
published by St. Anthony Messenger Press:

Book: *God Is Close to the Brokenhearted: Good News for Those Who Are Depressed*

Audiocassette: *Welcome Home, Healing Your Broken Heart*

Harvest Us Home

Good News as We Age

Rachel Callahan, C.S.C.
and
Rea McDonnell, S.S.N.D.

ST. ANTHONY MESSENGER PRESS

Cincinnati, Ohio

Unless otherwise noted, Scripture quotations are Rea McDonnell's own translation.

We are grateful for permission to quote material printed by the following publishers:

Reprinted by permission of Simon & Schuster and Curtis Brown, Ltd., *Fountain of Age* by Betty Friedan, copyright ©1993, originally published by Simon & Schuster. Reprinted by permission of Sister Dorothy A. Cahill, C.S.C., "Tempus" by Sister Dorothy A. Cahill C.S.C., in *Weavings*, January/February 1999. Reprinted by permission of The Liturgical Press, Collegeville, Minnesota, "You Are There," by Julie Howard, copyright Order of St. Benedict. Reprinted by permission of Warner Bros. Publications, Inc., "Take My Hand, Precious Lord," by Thomas Dorsey, copyright Warner Bros. Publications, Inc. Reprinted by permission of HarperCollins Publishers, *Anam Cara: A Book of Celtic Wisdom*, by John O'Donohue, copyright ©1997. Reprinted by permission of Farrar, Straus & Giroux. Inc., *Charming Billy*, by Alice McDermott, copyright ©1998. Reprinted by permission of Continuum Publishing Group, *Friends of God and Prophets*, by Elizabeth Johnson, copyright ©1998. Reprinted by permission of Ballantine Books, *Songs of Experience: An Anthology of Literature on Growing Old*, by Margaret Fowler and Priscilla McCutcheon, copyright ©1996. Reprinted by permission of W.W. Norton & Company, *After the Stroke*, copyright ©1988, and *The House by the Sea*, copyright ©1981, by May Sarton. Reprinted by permission of A.M. Heath & Company, Ltd. on behalf of the Estate of the Late May Sarton, *After the Stroke* published by The Women's Press (UK) in 1988 and *The House by the Sea* published by The Women's Press (UK) in 1996, by May Sarton.

Cover design by Constance M. Wolfer
Book design by Sandy L. Digman
Electronic pagination and format by Sandy L. Digman

ISBN 0-86716-372-0

Copyright ©2000, Congregation of the Holy Cross and School Sisters of Notre Dame

Published by St. Anthony Messenger Press

www.AmericanCatholic.org

Printed in the U.S.A.

W e dedicate this book to ALL OUR SISTERS and
      to ALL THOSE WHO HAVE MENTORED US
in our aging, especially Sister Loretto Conway, C.S.C., and
in loving memory of Armand (Manda) Adams,
Rose J. Irving, Sister Philemon Langhals, S.S.N.D.,
Sister Mary Paulina St. Amour, S.S.N.D.,
and John J. Shechan.

Contents

Introduction

Pope John Paul II proclaimed the year 2000 as *"Giubileo,"* a Jubilee Year. The fiftieth year in our biblical tradition is a holy year, the year of jubilee. At the beginning of his public ministry, Jesus proclaims a "year of the Lord's favor" (Luke 4:19), the coming of jubilee in his own person. Jubilee was a time when the people of Israel were to set captives free, to return to their homeland, to recover and reclaim their roots and family.

> ...you shall hallow the fiftieth year and proclaim liberation in the land for all its inhabitants. You shall make this your year of jubilee. All shall return to their own land and to their family. The fiftieth year shall be your jubilee. You shall not sow, and you shall not harvest the crop, nor shall you gather in the grapes...because it is jubilee, to be kept holy by you.... If slaves are not redeemed in the intervening years, then slaves and their children are to be released in the year of jubilee. (Leviticus 25:10-12, 54)

Paraphrasing this passage, Maria Harris highlights God's instruction to us about jubilee:

> You shall let the land lie fallow, that is, you shall
> practice Sabbath;
> You shall forgive debts, letting forgiveness in;
> You shall free captives and proclaim liberty;
> You shall find out what belongs to whom and give
> it back....
> You shall hold a great feast, learning to sing the canticle
> of "Jubilate." (*Proclaim Jubilee*, pages 2-3)

In keeping with this tradition, we proclaim good news for those in their fiftieth year and beyond. By our own personal fiftieth year, the mid-life crisis, if indeed there was one, is probably past. More fallow years lie ahead as we begin what we hope will be a more leisurely sabbath time of life.

In her article "Resting Reaping Times," Wendy Wright writes about lying fallow during a year of sabbatical:

> What has been new, to my surprise, has been the hidden, regenerative process of old wounds and ancient habits of being rising to the surface. Being exposed. Made conscious. My heart, my mind, my soul, turned over, laid bare. Fallowness has meant not only rest, but the uncovering of all that is lifeless and infertile in me. (page 11)

When our life is "turned over, laid bare" we may well discover debts that others owe us that we can only now forgive. Perhaps the greatest blessing is that we may gradually learn to forgive ourselves. As we dig up "all that is lifeless and infertile" we may experience some emotional pain, but it is the pain of captives being set free, coming from the depths of a dungeon into light for the first time in years. And we shall be invited to the great feast. We proclaim Sunday after Sunday, "We believe in the resurrection of the dead." This is good news.

Our own jubilee years are a time for lying fallow, however, not a time for working to bring in the harvest. We ask God to work, to harvest us. Saint Paul's image is helpful here, seeing us as the "field of God" (1 Corinthians 3:9) or the "garden of God." First we ask God to clear the ground of our hearts, hearts plowed up by the losses, rejections, deprivations of the human condition. Painful though this process of reviewing our lives may be, we can hear God's promise: "Come back, live in peace and you will be safe. Your strength lies in stillness and staying quiet" (Isaiah 30:15). It is God who clears, God who prepares the soil of our lives by turning over, fertilizing and sowing the seed who is Christ deep in our hearts. It is not our work. Again God promises: "I have made you, and it is I who will bear the burden. I will carry you to safety..." (Isaiah 46:4). It is God, of course, who grows us up into the fullness of Christ, watering and tending, shining the sunlight of Christ into our darkest places. All this is God's work (Ephesians 2:8).

We are called to cooperate with God's gardening. We have to attend to ourselves, our relationships, our memories, our futures. Throughout this book we look to Jesus as our pioneer in all that it means to be human, fully human and fully alive. We, like him, want to grow in wisdom and grace as we age. He certainly bore fruit in his public ministry. We can continue to be generative even into oldest age. We also turn to his mother, Mary, as one who can lead us into the joys and sorrows of living into our elder years. In fact, the chapter on Mary is the centerpiece of this book.

Both Jesus and Mary were "acquainted with suffering." In our image of ourselves as God's field, we know that we have been weeded and pruned frequently throughout our lives. As we come close to God's harvesting us home, we may enjoy good health and a deep, rich spiritual fertility. Or, God's pruning may take on a new intensity, a seeming diminishment of what seems most human of us. Thus we begin our own gathering in of all that is "...prized and passes of us, everything that's fresh and fast flying of us, seems to us sweet of us..." as Gerard Manley Hopkins, Jesuit poet of the nineteenth century, termed it. Yet the final harvest is God's work, and God harvests home the deepest beauty of us, as Hopkins phrases it in "The Leaden Echo and the Golden Echo." "...back to God, beauty's self and beauty's giver...."

As Christians in the second half of life, we may be able to blaze a trail of hope for our secular society, of a deeper acceptance of death, of a more profound understanding of resurrection in this new century. For many people the prospect (or the reality) of an empty nest, retirement from work and especially looming illness and death leads to denial, avoidance and depression. Anthropologist Ernest Becker, in his Pulitzer-prize-winning book entitled *The Denial of Death*, indicted American culture in particular of this blight. Immersed as we are in this culture, we need good news as we age.

Rachel will be sixty-one when this book is released and Rea, fifty-eight. "You are too young!" cried Sister Hester Valentine, S.S.N.D., when Rea told her of our project. One of Rea's former teachers, Sister Hester has written *Aging in the Lord* (Paulist, 1994), from her mid-eighties vantage point. She details a wide variety of nitty-gritty realities for the elderly. We admit we are newcomers to aging. But in a society that often neglects, ignores and even abuses its elders, we are convinced that our Christian faith, hope and love can heal some of the pain in the aging process. Our book, we hope, will help all those over fifty to age with more peace, joy and even anticipation, because we are daily convinced that in our aging, God is growing us, harvesting us, calling us home.

Our credentials include psychology studies for Rachel and Scripture studies for Rea. Rachel has twenty-seven years of practice, listening to stories of others' aging in therapy sessions. Rea has listened as a spiritual director for the past twenty-five years and as a pastoral counselor for the past eleven. More importantly, Rachel has experienced one death after another of her loved ones throughout her life. And Rea has a body that at thirty-nine had the osteoarthritis of a seventy-year-old; at forty-six, degenerative disk disease; cataract surgery on both eyes at fifty-four; and at fifty-six was diagnosed with yet another disease of the elderly, chronic lymphocytic leukemia.

One of our first revelations that we were aging happened on a downtown street in Ottawa, Ontario. When Rea was a mere forty-four and Rachel, forty-seven, some teenagers fooling around as they walked were suddenly warned by one of their mates: "Watch out! Don't knock into those old women." Once we began to write this book, the symbols of aging surrounded us. For example, this autumn is laden with golden leaves; as I, Rea, walked the dog I suddenly was showered in gold. The trees will stay tall and still in their kaleidoscope colors for a while, unless a storm shakes them from their leafhold. So will many of us stand tall unless debilitating ill health shakes us.

As you age, as we age, all of us who consider ourselves on the other half of mid-life, in this jubilee season, we "ponder in our hearts" all that God has done in our "one and only life."

Numerous books are being written today about aging—sociological, psychological, medical, philosophical studies. We have included some of them in our bibliography and will certainly include some of their facts and wisdom. We have also listened to the voices of our friends who are further along in aging, some whose writing about their journey is included. We are especially grateful to our friends who minister to the elderly, especially Barbara Mansfield. For the sustained metaphor of God's growing us, God's field, we needed, and are grateful for, the expertise of gardeners Joe Skeffington and Mary Elizabeth Kenel. We also are thankful for computer help from Jack McDonnell and Katie Mindling, R.S.M., and the support and printer of Camilla Fitzgerald, C.S.C. Thank you, too, to all who contributed their stories.

This book is not a compendium of aging. Our hope in writing this book is invitational. We invite you to reflect upon good news, upon God's good work in you. Harvesting is a process, not an event. So during these autumn days of our lives, as our good God quietly, gently and sometimes not so gently, harvests us home, we want to be attentive to how the good news of God's love for and in the world is being made flesh in us as we age.

This is not a book to be read in a single sitting, nor even necessarily in sequential order. Different portions and certainly different exercises will speak to you at different moments. Be guided by the wisdom of your own Spirit working in you.

We are not alone in this journey no matter how alone and lonely the journey may seem at times. God promises to be with us. In a particular way we invite Mary our Mother to be with us. While we don't know historical particulars, there is good reason to believe that Mary made the journey into old age, one that Jesus was cut off from by premature death.

We hope this book will be a prayer pilgrimage for you, allowing you to savor some of the mysteries of grace that you have lived. We pray that each person who reads this book may "see what hope God's call holds for you" (Ephesians 1:18). With Saint Paul we are confident "that the One who began this good work in you will bring it to completion" (Philippians 1:6).

Easter Season, 1999
Silver Spring, Maryland

PART ONE

A HARVEST IS THE CULMINATION OF A LONG PROCESS. *God's harvesting us, gathering us in, begins with a clearing of the ground for the first planting. We begin with the good news that as we head for home, God's own self, God has always been at work deep within our being to clear and plow, to plant and tend, to harvest us—finally—home. Saint Catherine of Siena wrote: "All the way to heaven is heaven"; in this book we will spell out the good news that all the way home to God is God. "It is all God's doing"* (EPHESIANS 2:8).

CHAPTER ONE

Clearing the Ground

The gospel, the Christian Good News, begins with a call to repentance, to a change of attitude and a change of heart. We begin each Eucharist with a confession of both our sin and our trust in God's faithful and tender mercy. God who has begun good work in us from our mothers' wombs is continually in the process of clearing, plowing, sowing and growing us into the fullness of Christ. Does God ever finish sowing the seed of Christ, of God's life which is grace, in us? How does this planting occur as we age?

The first step in planting is to clear the ground. Saint Paul has named us as God's good earth: "You are God's field" (1 Corinthians 3:9). In some ways all of our life's work is clearing the ground. "Prepare the way for the Lord," cried John the Baptist, the austere cousin of Jesus, who spent his adult life in the emptiness of the desert. Not many of us are called to the radical, wild barrenness of a real desert, but most of us have had the paradoxical experience of meeting God in the wilderness of our own desert spaces deep within. Not many of us will experience the martyrdom of the Baptist, but each of us is a martyr (meaning "witness" in Greek), testifying that God is with us moment by moment as we grow in wisdom, age and grace.

The clearing of the ground that God invites us to in this second half of our life may be as dramatic as a call to the desert or martyrdom. More probably, however, it is a gradual and gentle emptying of all that clutters our life. In her beautiful spiritual classic *The Reed of God*, Caryll Houselander writes of this process of emptying. She identifies emptying as the beginning of contemplation, the kind of contemplation that each of us ordinary, Christ-bearing humans are called to by our Baptism. This contemplation is not just for monastics. Contemplation is a clearing: seeing reality with more clarity and hearing the voice of God in all creation more clearly. Contemplation, writes Jesuit Walter Burghardt, is our long, loving look at the real.

Emptying

We live in an age when many suffer barren lives, lives devoid of meaning. We may have futilely tried to fill the space with noise or things or busyness. This is not the emptiness that Houselander describes. She highlights rather the hollow, receptive emptiness that allows us to receive the fullness of the life and love of God. We are the "earthen vessels," each of us unique in gift and life experience, all of us united as loved sinners upon whom God wants to lavish divine fullness. We are, as she phrases it, "the reed of God," the hollowed pipe through which the music of God can fill the world.

Let us begin by inviting the Spirit to show us what needs to be cleared from our land right now:

For Reflection and Prayer

Take some time to imagine the "ground" of your interior right now. Is it a level field? Or a rocky, rugged hillside? Is it dry red clay, cracked and thirsty? Is it a cluttered backyard or a manicured front lawn? Imagine your inner ground as graphically as you can. What's "growing" now in your ground? If you keep a journal you might write, draw or paint your "ground." Is your ground soft or hard these days? What treasures may lie hidden deep within your ground? What do you hope might be uncovered deep within you?

We must clear the ground of obvious obstacles to growth even before we plow. But if God clears the ground, we can be assured that this is not a harsh and ruthless clearing. We need to reverence the shoots of life and the hidden treasures beneath the surface.

In the middle of the twentieth century, theologian Paul Tillich named God the ground of our being. Even earlier, in the late 1800's, Gerard Manley Hopkins, in his poem "The Wreck of the Deutschland," imaged God as the ground of all human being: "Ground of being, and granite of it: past all/Grasp God...."

God is mystery, past any grasping or defining or absolutizing by theologians or churchmen or any of us. Past-all-grasp-God instead is the one who grasps us, not to clutch, but to hold us steady. "I stretch forward," writes Saint Paul, "to grasp hold of Christ who has already grasped hold of me" (Philippians 3:14). What security! God grounds us, is the ground "in which we live and move and have our being" (Acts 17:28). Ground of all human being, of all creation. We, all of creation, are joined at the root. All are pulled by gravity to the center, who is God. All are held steady and together. And God is the granite of our being, our rock. Even if, as we age, we grow more unsteady physically, more shaky in memory, more vulnerable, closer to tears, God is the granite of our being. "Think of the rock you were quarried from" (Isaiah 51:1).

God as Ground of Our Being

Don't worry if your ground is hard or rocky. God is the granite of our being. We need not dynamite the bedrock. God is the bedrock under our own stubborn hardness or rocky sinfulness. God can send shoots of new life through the ground of our being, and does—daily.

Suppose the soil of our life seems worn out with bearing: Bearing sorrow, loss, grief; bearing neglect, insults, insecurity; bearing others' burdens, not so much to "fulfill the law of Christ" (Galatians 6:2), but because we had to, or felt we had to, or there was no one else to shoulder the burden. If God clears the ground of our life, under the fallen leaves and brambles of bearing too much for too long, some new, rich and fertile earth will be discovered.

Suppose our soil is acidic, like our personalities: sharp and critical, a humor that slices our own self and others, a cynical viewpoint on every topic. "My heart grew parched as stubble in a summer drought," cried the psalmist (Psalm 32:4). A pulling away from social contact lest we burn others and ourselves with the acid of our bitter hearts, from which the mouth speaks. As God clears our hearts, the sunshine can sweeten the depths of our interior lives, even in the very oldest age. To say that because a person is old, she or he cannot change is an evil untruth. With God we are always in the process of being and becoming ever more Christ. Saint Paul writes: "Where the Spirit of the Lord is, there is freedom.... We are always being transformed into the image of Christ, from glory to glory. Such is the influence of the Spirit" (2 Corinthians 3:17-18). Even at eighty or ninety, daily being transformed into Christ, we are still only learning to say: "It is no longer I who live, but Christ lives in me" (Galatians 2:20).

The ground of everyone's interior is littered. Some of our memories need healing, some of our relationships need sorting through, some hidden crevices house pain or rage that must yet see the light. We will continue this life review throughout this whole book. If you have never kept a journal, we suggest that you start now, recording your thoughts, feelings, dreams, drawings in privacy. A simple pad of paper will do.

The Spirit, working through our imaginations in the exercise above, has shown us the shape of our ground. We have some idea of the soil, the clay, the rock of ourselves with which we and God, our farmer, will work together. It is hard work, but beneath the soil, always supporting us, is God, our bedrock, the ground of our being and granite of it.

CHAPTER TWO

Preparing the Ground

We have asked the Spirit to show us the shape of our ground, to help us know what might need to be emptied or cleared. We have begun. With reverence for the soil of our interior, God and we have set aside the litter, at least that discovered thus far. We may be ready now for the plow.

Plowing the Ground

What does the word *plow* conjure up? Is it a noun or a verb? Depending upon where we live and the time of the year during which we are reading this, we may picture a sod breaker or a snow plow. Or we may think of *plow* as a verb: plowing ahead, clearing away every obstacle; plowing into, conjuring relentless force; plowing on, putting that "one foot in front of the other" that we must sometimes force ourselves to do just to get through a day. Like so many words in our language the word *plow* is colored by our personal experience. It may evoke positive or fearful feelings. We invite you to use the image of plowing in a gentle way. God does not want a harsh and determined turning over of the ground of our lives; rather a more careful tilling is called for.

For Reflection and Prayer

Whatever your feelings or past experiences of being "plowed up," turned over, broken, take some time now to let God be with you in those feelings. Then listen to the good news from Scripture about how tenderly God plows:

You care for the land, watering the fields,
making them rich and fertile.
You ready the seeds, prepare the grain.
You abundantly send rain on plowed fields
and soak them with water.
You soften the soil with water,
gently breaking up the clods of earth. (Psalm 65:9-10)

Your imaging in Chapter One was of your interior life as ground, grounded in the ground of all being, God. Now image yourself as that field of Psalm 65, perhaps full of stones, maybe even boulders and stumps that the plow has overturned. What are some of the stones, boulders, stumps, clods that still litter the field of your life?

Take God (Jesus/Spirit/Mary) on a tour of your field. What do they see? Speak freely of how you feel, but listen to them tell you the good news in and about your field, about the treasure hidden there.

God, Our Gentle Farmer

When Jesus images God as a vinedresser in John 15:1, the Greek word in the Gospel, *georgos*, actually means farmer. God is our farmer. As we turn over the fields of our own lives we need to exercise reverence and care. We plow the ground by hand and heart, not with mechanical steel scrapers or claws of iron. God initiates the plowing. We, in a dialogue and a dance of God's action and our response, break up the clods of our own life, with all the love and care that we are able to muster. God, our good gardener (Isaiah 35), guides this initial experience of life review.

For Reflection and Prayer

Image our farmer God stooping to you, smiling, to pick up a clod of earth from your field. Notice how this good farmer doesn't smash the clump, but breaks it open to the sunshine. Is there a clod or a clump of something knotted in you? Hand it to God (Jesus/Spirit/Mary). Watch the knot dissolve into small and malleable pieces in the hand of God.

Now God stoops again to integrate the opened chunk of dirt into the
field. How does this feel to you? Do you have another clump to offer
God? Or do you just want to rest in the peace of a knot loosened, a
clod softened and broken open?

Life Review

Life review, both of the tightened, crusty chunks in our hearts
or of the rich, fertile and open earth of our interior field, is an
important task of growing older. It can be done yearly. Some of
us make a practice of reviewing our entire life on the last day of
each year, or on our birthday, to prepare for the year ahead. It
becomes a personal jubilee day to return to the land we came
from; to let the captives in our hearts—our fears, our
resentments, our hungers, our hurts—go free; to forgive debts;
to experience year after year that we are forgiven. Eugene
Bianchi cautions that life review is truly a recollection, not just
telling stories of the good old days (*On Growing Older*, page 26).
In our collecting again the graces and sorrows of our life, and
perhaps journaling about the feelings that arise when
recollecting, we become as the psalmist described: "fields filled
with flocks...valleys full of wheat" (Psalm 65:12-13).

God is farmer, and much that God has plowed up is to
make way for nourishing foods. Some fields are full of
vegetables and grains, but others are full of flowers. Flowers
nurture another part of the human being. Jesus himself
contemplated the lilies of the fields. God is also a gardener, able
to make the desert bloom.

> Let the wilderness and parched land rejoice!
> Let the desert ring gladness and burst into flower!
> It flowers with fields of blossoms....
> Waters spring up in the wilderness,
> Torrents flow through the desert,
> Grass grows in the rough land.... (Isaiah 35:1-2, 6-7)

For the people of Israel, for Jesus and Mary, the desert breaking
into bloom was a nearby wonder. We don't have to visit the
deserts of our Southwest to understand. Haven't we been just

as surprised by joy, finding life and new growth in the most unexpected places? Flowers sprout in the crevice of a rock. The dead wood of a fallen tree hosts the new life of a seedling. Pebbles and gravel along the roadside are unable to stifle the pinks and whites and golds of the wildflowers that grow willy-nilly along the way. Even indoors, a plant we have forgotten to water, droopy and brown, springs back to life with just a bit of attention. As we carefully turn over the pieces of our own life, the stony places, the apparently dead places, as well as the rich, fertile places, let us ask God that we may find life.

> How kind you are, God, to your land...
> Your saving presence remains steady in our land.
> Glory fills our land.
> Kindness and faithfulness meet, justice and peace embrace.
> Faithfulness sprouts from the earth. (Psalm 85:1, 9-11)

Fertilizing the Earth

As Saint Paul writes in his own life review to the community in Philippi (Philippians 3:4-14), he counts all his religious credentials and considerable spiritual accomplishments as so much dung, manure, garbage, for the sake of knowing Christ Jesus. Organic gardeners believe that the only real way to practice sustainable agriculture is to grow soil, not plants. Plants are a byproduct. How could the field ever be ripe for harvest without the decay that has fertilized the soil? There is the natural decay of microscopic life fallen in the field. The ecologically concerned collect vegetable scraps near their kitchen sinks to make compost to fertilize their kitchen gardens; others use natural animal dung or processed fertilizers. Just so, there is a mix of refuse and manure in our own lives.

Let us image our personal compost heap. Here the failures, the sins, the regrets, the hurts, the resentments, the worries of our entire life lie, decaying, perhaps festering. Compost heaps may contain coffee grounds; as in our lives, what once added flavor is used up now and cast aside. Sometimes there are inedible greens and stalks, as in our life we have spit out or cut off what cannot nourish us. Sometimes there are the pits and rinds of fruits, the remnants of what has nourished us. Sometimes we add fragile eggshells, or even our own hair and nails, rich in calcium and nitrogen. But it will all decay and smell—and give life again.

Jesus tells a story in Luke's Gospel of how important fertilizing is to growth.

A man had a vineyard in which he had planted a fig tree. He came looking for fruit from it, but there was none. So he said to the vinedresser: "It has been three years that I have been looking for fruit and not finding any. Cut the tree down. Why let it spoil the ground?" The vinedresser said: "Sir, let it go one more year until I have dug around it and thrown dung on it. If it produces fruit in the future, good. And if not, you shall cut it down." (Luke 13:6-9)

If we, like the younger Saint Paul, have been afraid all our life that we have not won God's approval, if we have spent a lifetime working for merit and grace, working to earn a heavenly reward, then we may be afraid to see ourselves as we are. We may gag on the words of the tax collector in Jesus' parable of the Pharisee and the sinner who begs, "God, be merciful to me, a sinner" (Luke 18:9-14). Just as our society denies death, so many of us tend to deny sin and weakness and failure. Like Paul, we may have to be converted from our goodness. We may even, like Paul, learn to boast of our weakness: "...[Christ] said to me, 'My grace is enough for you. My power is made perfect in weakness.' So I will gladly boast rather of my weaknesses, so that the power of Christ might overshadow me...for when I am weak, then I am full of power" (2 Corinthians 12:9-10).

Perhaps like the vinedresser digging around the fig tree, we may uncover for the first time our sin and weakness. Perhaps the memories of some sin are only too fresh. But, we beg you, do not use a Brillo pad on your already bruised heart. Do not scour your past, obsessing about your guilt and shame. Let Christ do the work, let him make his power perfect in your weakness. Instead of examining yourself, ask the Holy Spirit to teach you—to teach you your sin. No one else knows your sin. Your family and friends, and especially your enemies, may think they know well your sins. They judge you, and you may have internalized their judgments, especially the judgments of your parents when you were younger.

The Spirit, however, will be most courteous, gentle, kind in teaching you to yourself. Good teachers do not overwhelm their students with too much information, so this revelation of you to yourself will be gradual. It may not happen during a quiet time of prayer, nor during an examination of conscience. It may contradict what your parents said was your sin or wayward ways; it may even contradict what you yourself would judge as sin. You may be surprised that what you thought was sinful is not, and what the Spirit teaches you is sin is a revelation to you.

Here is a simple prayer to begin each day: "Holy Spirit, do not let me deny the truth today. Teach me my sin." This prayer is meant only for the fertilizing period as you work through this book. If we are tempted to deny truth, we might pray daily the first half of the prayer. Too much focus on our sin, however, can be narcissistic. God needs our energy focused most of the time on the grace, not the sin, in our lives. "Where sin abounds, grace more abounds," writes Paul (Romans 5:20).

"Give me one more year," the vinedresser in the parable pleads. This is the year, now is the acceptable time to review how we have been fertilized.

For Reflection and Prayer

What is the dung in your life? If you can, find a bowl, preferably earthenware or rusty or chipped. Set it before you. You will need a container to hold this dung. First, let us consider the dung that was just thrown around you, like the fig tree in Jesus' parable. What has happened in your life that was deadly, decaying, smelly, even maggoty? Was it the early loss of a parent, a learning disability, a rumor spread about you, an unfair boss, being "let go" from a job, a disease—something out of your control, just thrown at you like so much manure? You might want to jot down a list. Then...invite Jesus to come to you. Watch him in your imagination as he picks up the bowl you have set before you. Take each of these pains that you have remembered, hold it up before him and you, and with him consider the manure of your life. Will he ask you to deposit each hurt in the bowl, or will he get his own hand dirty as he holds it out to receive all that you might judge as ugly and smelly? Let this imagining develop as the Spirit leads...

Our Own Compost Heap

The dung happened. It was flung at you. The compost heap is our own project. Coffee grounds, stalks and greens, pits and rinds, egg shells. Let us use the same process in this time of fertilizing the soil of our lives.

For Reflection and Prayer

What is in the compost heap of your life? What once added flavor and now is used up, discarded? A relationship milked dry? Your arthritic leg joints? What has been cut off and spit out because it offers no nourishment? A job? A disillusionment with your parent/spouse/ child/friend/church/God? What are the pits and rinds, the remnants of what once was so nourishing? The memories of loved ones gone to God or to the other side of the country? The inability to get enough rest? The music you can no longer play? Where are the fragile pieces of your life? The bits of your own self cut off? A tentative love? A doubt of God's love for you? Regrets about your marriage? You might journal about these heartaches and losses, or make a simple list. Then invite Jesus to reach out to take and caress each piece in your compost heap. Because of his touch, the decay can be transformed into what will give life. There is no need to be ashamed of any event, feeling, sin, even anger or disappointment with God. Jesus will accept everything you offer him.

Jesus had another parable about accepting ourselves just the way we are, even just the way we were. It is the story of the man who planted a field, but his enemy crept in at night to sow weeds among the wheat sprouts (Matthew 13:24-30). The field workers in the parable might remind us of ourselves, zealous to root up every weed from the field, from our life. The master is wiser, however, for he doesn't want to risk even a single grain of wheat that might be plucked up along with the weeds. He instructs the servants—and us—to let the weeds grow along with the wheat. Then when all is cut down and gathered in at harvesttime, it will be easy to separate the weeds from the wheat.

Once again we are reminded that we dare not judge ourselves, let alone anyone else. How do we know what is the weed and what the wheat of our life? What we might count as our good works, our spiritual accomplishments and rights, might be merely chaff in God's eyes. What in ourselves we judge so harshly might be the very sin which makes us so loveable in God's eyes. For example, Saint Mechtilde, a nun in Saint Gertrude's medieval convent, was worn down by Abbess Gertrude's short temper. When she begged God to make her friend more patient, God replied that Gertrude's repentance was far more pleasing than her patience.

The parable of the weeds among the wheat reinforces what Paul first experienced and then taught. We are not to take our spiritual pulse, let alone root about the field with a sharp scythe. Only the Spirit knows our sin. Only the Spirit can weed our field, only God can prune the branches. But what trust to let God do the sorting out on judgment day!

Trust is the biblical meaning of faith. Faith, as we find the word in Scripture, has little to do with intellectual assent to divinely revealed truths. Faith is a matter of the trusting heart, not the well-schooled head. The faith that is trust, however, is the faith that saves. Trusting God, clinging to God, commitment to God are all meanings of biblical faith.

So it is with a trusting spirit that we have dared to notice what is in our own compost heap. Noticing is a quiet, gentle activity. This kind of noticing requires neither 20/20 vision nor perfectly acute hearing. It does require an awareness and a listening heart.

As we gently scan the compost of our own lives we want to pay attention to our feelings. Most of us have lived long enough to know that feelings come and go. If once we were taught that feelings of anger, fear, doubt, sexuality, even depression were sins, now we know that they are neither bad nor good. Feelings

14

just are, and are an important part of what makes us human beings. Feelings are morally neutral. They are gifts of God and helpful signals to us to look more deeply at what triggers a particular feeling.

Awareness of feelings adds to the richness of life. Yet if we have been exposed to repeated painful experiences of our own and/or others' feelings, especially early in life, our beings have the built-in self-protective mechanisms that allowed us then to defend ourselves, especially against too much pain. Those defenses were helpful. Today, we simply are where we are—perhaps both full of feeling, and defended against feeling. Genesis tells us: "And God saw that it was good." We, each of us and all of us, God's creation, are good.

If physical pain or chronic ache has us by the throat, however, we may be able to notice only these bodily realities of now. For example, as we are writing this book, the ninety-eight-year-old to whom it is dedicated, Sister Loretto, is worn down with congestive heart failure, which makes even breathing a chore. Her most acute awareness is the "now" of a dense weariness. She who has been both bright and wise all her life can hardly feel anything and certainly can't examine defenses. "I can't pray or even think," she recently said. And God is in her weariness, struggling for breath with her, although she is barely able to whisper the Our Father.

For us, however, today might be the time to reflect, a time to notice an unexpected epiphany in our personal compost heap, to be surprised by a joyful sight, sound, taste, memory, sense of meaning in whatever our ache. As poet/novelist/journal-keeper May Sarton wrote in her older age:

> We have to keep the channels in ourselves open to pain. At the same time it is essential that true joys be experienced, that the sunrise not leave us unmoved, for civilization depends on the true joy, all those that have nothing to do with money or affluence—nature, the arts, human love.
> (*The House by the Sea*, page 25)

Whatever we notice today, let us notice without judgment. Remember the field of both weed and wheat that was described

15

earlier in this chapter. God does the judging. Because we are unable to comprehend the vastness of God's love, we are probably in for some wonderful surprises.

Earlier in this chapter we invited you to journal. Journaling, pouring out thoughts and feelings uncensored, either in words or with other artistic expression, is a powerful tool to process and integrate what we discover in our life experience. Sharing pieces of our very private journal with another: sibling, spouse, friend, spiritual director or counselor can be a further way to appreciate some of what we have lived, our own experience. Now we deliberately return to an exercise from the beginning of this chapter. If you worked it through then, with or without a journal, working it again will most likely show you how journaling can take you ever deeper into the mystery who is you.

For Reflection and Prayer

What is in the compost heap of your life? What once added flavor and now is used up, discarded? What has been cut off and spit out because it offers no nourishment? What are the pits and rinds, the remnants of what once was so nourishing? Where are the fragile pieces of your life?

Once again, journal about these heartaches and losses; once again, make a simple list. Then invite Jesus to take and caress each piece in your compost heap. Because of his touch, the decay can be transformed into what will give life. There is no need to be ashamed of any event, feeling, sin, even anger or disappointment with God. Jesus will accept everything you offer him.

Learning From Others

We recommend reading the journals of others, especially those who have grown old well, to find encouragement. Novels, films and short stories can also throw an unexpected searchlight upon our life experiences, particularly those that may be too vast and/or horrible to contemplate in detail. For example, some World War II films such as *Saving Private Ryan* and *A Thin Red Line* do not spare us from the horrors of war. A forceful, bestselling novel, *Bird Song* by Sebastian Faulks, brings us viscerally into the trenches of No Man's Land in World War I. Sometimes questions raised in books or films give voice and focus to our own questions that may feel too big to handle. For example, *Ordinary People* opens a depth of family pain that ordinary people may close off in denial. In identifying with the various characters, we can allow memories to surface, can replay scenes from our own life, can try out in our imagination some ways of doing or feeling that are/were not possible for us in reality.

It is hard to know whether constant exposure to media events dulls or expands our capacity for noticing. Yet powerful literature and art in whatever form can trigger feeling-memory, carry us beyond ourselves and into our own unnoticed experience in a way that is grace. As we age, building our own personal compost heap, we can understand what Saint Therese of Lisieux taught us: that in fact "everything is grace."

The Cultural Compost Heap

Depending upon the cultures in which you have lived, you may pick out from our brief survey different bits and pieces to reflect upon.

For Reflection and Prayer

Reflect upon some of the realities that exist in whatever culture in which you find yourself. Take some time to notice the features of the culture in which you live, be it rich or poor, rural or urban, ethnically diverse or homogeneous. What are some of the assumptions of your particular culture about aging, beauty, suffering, having, doing? Take some time to jot your reflections.

When Betty Friedan was about to turn sixty, society's judgment on the elderly struck her numb. She admits: "It was not easy to break through my own denial of age. Pangs of doubt, pain, and fear kept erupting, clouding a vision of new freedom that I glimpsed, making me lose hold of that grounding in new reality—the affirmation of age on its own terms" (*Fountain of Age*, page 69).

Ageism. Recent decades have seen a spate of books and studies about aging. Medical advances and healthier life habits extend the life span of many in the first world. We have started to reflect upon the possibilities for growth in old age, on wellness in aging, rather than to focus mainly on diminishment. On the whole, however, the cultural messages about aging in the Western world have been less than positive. When Friedan was assembling material for *The Fountain of Age*, one of the pieces of data that she gathered was media images of aging. Usually the only time we see older persons in advertisements are in ads for dietary supplements, denture adhesive, medications or cosmetic camouflage of any physical signs of aging. Friedan contends that various negative myths about aging create prejudice and stereotypes. There is little recognition that as we age we become more and more our individual selves and hardly the homogenized clump called elderly. Grudging respect is tendered to the political clout of groups like the AARP. But calling this political advocacy group the "geezers from hell" simultaneously demeans while affirming its power.

Many cultures do have great regard for their elders, recognizing and seeking their wisdom, honoring their spiritual power. Their gray hair evokes respect, not pity. United States culture venerates youth, or at least the appearance of youth. While there is a healthy movement beginning to bud—to think about "age-ing" as "sage-ing"—for the most part our contemporary Western world does not give the same respectful recognition to elders that some of the Eastern cultures do.

In some places in the world today, people cherish a wrinkled face and even look forward to their first gray hairs. In the village of Vilcabamba in the Ecuadorean Andes, where people have exceptionally long life spans, some elders exaggerate their age to gain greater respect. In India, men and women look forward to old age as a time to detach from the obligations of work and family life to seek knowledge of the inner self. The Japanese, who regard old age as a source of prestige, celebrate a national holiday called "Honor the Aged Day." Native Americans think of their elders as wisdomkeepers whose contemplative skills help safeguard tribal survival. (Schachter-Shalomi, *Age-ing to Sage-ing*, pages 52-53)

Most of us are affected, however subtly, by the prejudices of the dominant culture. So we need not be surprised if we discover traces of ageism in ourselves as well as in the environment.

Denial of death. Another dimension of our cultural compost heap is the denial of death. In this culture, death and dying have not been considered a normal part of the process of life through the last half of the twentieth century. Medical breakthroughs in curing disease and repairing/replacing aging joints and organs push the horizon of natural death farther into the future as the average lifespan in the Western world is constantly revised upward. Anxiety about our own mortality is often hard to acknowledge.

May Sarton writes:

But by the time one is sixty there is deeper anxiety that has to be dealt with, and that is the fear of death, or rather, I should say, the fear of dying in some inappropriate or gruesome way, such as long illness requiring care. I sometimes actually sweat when I think of Tamas [her dog] should I fall and break my neck, Tamas unable to get out! Why talk about it? I say "talk about it" because these are the things we bury and never do bring it out into the open. And what is a journal for if they are never mentioned. (*House by the Sea*, page 53)

Later in this book we will invite you to ponder, we hope with less fear, the reality of death as a natural part of life. Our good God is harvesting us home and journeying with us in the process.

Beautiful equals young. Our society has cultural stereotypes about beauty. Depending upon the degree to which we internalize these, the more difficult the transition to the normal signs of aging, wrinkles, sags. It is fascinating to see how standards of beauty change. We just need to look at some of the "old" movies. The beauty queens of the 1940's and 1950's were more buxom than they are today. Hawaii is probably the only state in the Union where beauty contests are sequenced over a three-year period for different age groups, young, middle-aged and old.

Our religious tradition, on the other hand, values the beauty of old age:

> As the clear light is upon the holy candlestick,
> so is the beauty of the face in ripe age. (Ecclesiasticus 26:17)

In a society with so many products to counteract baldness or to color our hair, the Book of Proverbs announces: "Gray hair is a crown of glory!" (16:31).

"Having" and "doing." Another characteristic of our culture is consumerism. Some of us may have discovered that buying can reduce anxiety. While "shop till you drop" may indicate an unhealthy lack of freedom, for most of us shopping can be a relational activity, either enjoyed with another or in trying to find gifts for people we love. But shopping lists, shopping TV channels and our options keep growing. Having a lot of material things, the latest gadgets and so on, becomes a definition of status and worth. If possessing seems an issue for younger folks, we do have a certain realistic worry about sufficient resources for old age. This anxiety is shared by all except the very rich. Having does not equal happiness, but not needing to worry about money is for most a real blessing. Letting go, sharing what we have, rather than accumulating more might be the most critical invitation to conversion that our culture as a whole and each of us as individuals face.

Jesus has pioneered a freedom for us in this area. He noted that foxes had their dens, birds had nests, and yet he had nowhere to lay his head. He was dependent during his public ministry on the kindness of others to house and feed him: banquets, simple meals, homes of the rich, sleeping outdoors on the bare ground. Unlike most men of his culture, he had no children to care for him in his old age, so what might have been his fear for his future? If he is really human, and he is, he didn't have a crystal ball to foresee his crucifixion at so young an age. He preached more than any other words these four: "Do not be afraid." He was tempted like us in everything, including fear and anxiety. At some point, however, he must have let God free him, like the lilies of the field and the sparrows, from worry about his future material needs.

For Reflection and Prayer

Speak to Jesus now of your own financial and material worries. Then sit (or lie) quietly and listen for his reassurance.

Our society places more value on "doing" rather than on "being." This reality can be more problematic for men than for women in a culture where identity is determined by the job one does. Women, in juggling work and home roles, have often been required to learn flexibility and are less apt to confuse identity with a particular job. As medical science and healthy living extend our lifespan, there is a new invitation to value being, not simply doing.

These are only a few of the elements in our cultural compost heap. Take a little time to reflect upon what you might add and how these factors impact your own experience of aging.

The Religious Compost Heap

Before we leave our compost heap, we must examine some of the once-nourishing pieces of our religious belief and devotion, so that we might let Jesus touch and transform them. Human beings have a tendency to absolutize certain beliefs and practices, and absolutizing is at the core of mental illness, asserts William Lynch, S.J., in *Images of Hope*. You will best know your own rigidities. Let us spell out some that the Church has named as heresy and check whether our own belief is still tinged with these absolutes.

Jesus only "seems" human. Historically, the first heresy the Christian Church had to confront was Docetism, the teaching that Jesus was God in disguise, not really human, but only "seeming" (*dokeo* is "seem" in Greek) to be human. For example, after Jesus gave his "bread of life" discourse and many disciples would no longer walk with him, a Docetist would insist that when he turned to the Twelve and asked, "Will you go away too?" (John 6:67) he already knew Peter's response. He was just testing the apostles. Because he was God in human guise, Jesus therefore knew everything, and could do calculus in his head while waiting for Peter to answer. Not at all. Out to the compost heap!

Jesus was truly human and did not ask questions to test or trip people. His enemies did. Jesus asked questions because he sincerely wanted to know. He needed feedback so that he could know. For example, the blind man whom Jesus didn't cure well enough on his first attempt had to give him honest feedback or the poor man's condition—seeing men like trees walking— would be worse than seeing nothing (Mark 8:22-26). Jesus had to lay hands on him a second time.

Jesus asks us questions today. We might not hear a voice in our heads, but in our hearts we can hear him ask: "How are you today? How are you feeling? Anything you'd like to talk over with me? Tell me what you want today." The Docetist of today (just because a teaching is declared heresy, don't think it disappears!) would reply: "But Jesus knows everything so I don't have to tell him how I feel and what I want." If our free will is God's great gift to us, and if a part of our freedom is our privacy, then how would Jesus dare violate our privacy, invade our thoughts? We know he doesn't invade our hearts, but waits to be invited in, so why would he know what we are thinking and feeling unless we tell him? Many Christians know this intuitively, and married Christians know that expecting spouses to read minds can lead to trouble. In relationships that are important to us we share our ideas, desires and emotions; in other words, we communicate ourselves on a deep and deepening level. Jesus is a real human being who wants to be important to us, to know us and be known by us.

For Reflection and Prayer

Like the blind man, you may feel that there is something in your life that Jesus did not heal well enough the first time. Tell him what you think and feel and need from him. Don't be afraid. He will lay hands on you a second time. He will be glad to!

Misunderstanding of justice. Another heresy condemned in the second century is still with us. Marcion taught then that the God of the Jewish Scriptures was a God of justice (read: revenge, tyranny, punishment) and the God of the New Testament was a God of mercy. Marcion did not understand the Jewish word for justice, which is the same word for holiness. When Matthew records that Joseph was a just man for not having Mary killed for her supposed adultery, he means that Joseph is holy as God is holy. If Joseph were just in Marcion's system, Joseph would have carried out capital punishment on Mary.

The practical fallout from such an ancient heresy is that many Christians find the Jewish Scriptures somewhat suspect. What a sorrow, however, to miss the emotional riches of the prophets and psalmists as they loved and cried out and wrestled and sang with their God. To ignore the Jewish Scriptures is to deprive oneself of the vitality of God's faithfulness and tender kindness, the very way that our God is holy. This book will rely heavily on the psalms as a way to get more of our whole self involved with God. Our minds, our hearts, and every human feeling are expressed to God in them.

Dualism. Dualism is just about worn out enough for the compost heap. Dualism is not actually false doctrine, a heresy. Rather dualism is merely a system of Western thought through which much of Christian doctrine was expressed. When early Christianity, which was so Jewish in thought and feeling, was brought to the Greek-thinking world, Greek ideas prevailed over the more holistic Jewish experience of God. Four common examples of a dualistic split often used in our Christian theology: matter/spirit; body/soul; an abstract Supreme Being/a feeling, dancing God; this world/the other world. A more modern example: young/old, youth/the elderly.

The trouble with dualistic thinking is that it seems that when we human beings have only two to choose between, one item is put on a pedestal and the other is demonized. So if the spirit is good, then the matter that drags it down must be bad, must be fought against, despised, discarded. If the soul is good, the body tends to be understood as bad. If God's perfection meant that God never changes and is beyond all passion, then to worship God with feeling and dancing becomes suspect. While the Eastern Christian churches have always held that God is constantly changing, is indeed uncreated energy, our Western idea of God, unfortunately, is that God transcends change and that God spurns all feeling.

Perfectionism. Christians were taught to try to be "perfect." In a dualistic system that might mean to transcend the body, its flesh, sexuality, emotion. For Luke's Jesus, on the other hand, perfection was about growing in wisdom, grace and compassion. "Be you compassionate as your heavenly Father is compassionate" (Luke 6:36). Perfectionism as denying or even stomping down our feelings and our body does plague some of us interiorly. Perfectionism can also lead us to judge others.

Our need to be perfect, religiously perfect even if we weren't A students, college athletes, or didn't have wealthy or successful parents, recalls Paul's need to be perfect. In keeping the Law (and he meant the 637 Jewish laws) he was perfect. Not only did he think that he would win God's favor, but he was proud of his accomplishment. This is a dualistic splitting that cancels our trust in God. We come to believe that we can achieve religious perfection ourselves. It has cropped up in every age, as Manichaeism in Augustine's time and as Jansenism in the eighteenth century, which still has a toehold in today's spirituality.

Dualism's splitting might blind us to the truth of our sinfulness—"If we say we have no sin, we deceive ourselves" (1 John 1:8). We try to hide our sin and weakness away, from

24

others for fear of their judgment, from ourselves because we judge ourselves lacking. Yet Jesus keeps on announcing: "I have come for the sick; the healthy have no need of a physician" (Matthew 9:12).

Denial of weakness. Our society tends to discard the weak and powerless. Like Paul's Corinthian community, many of us may find the powerlessness of Jesus just as much a stumbling block as did the first-century Jews, may find the weakness of Jesus just as much stupidity as did the first-century Greeks. Yet Paul wanted to preach Christ, not the wonderworker, but the crucified. Paul did not use "eloquent wisdom" lest the cross of Christ be emptied of its power. "For the message of the cross," he asserts, "is foolishness to those who are perishing, but to us who are being saved, the cross is the very power of God" (1 Corinthians 1:17-25). We who build up our social credentials and powerful connections, boast of our wealth and fame, might prefer to be identified with the powerful Son of God rather than with the sweaty, tormented man from Nazareth stumbling on his way to crucifixion. It is hard to look on the powerlessness of God embodied in Jesus. Our looking away may stem from fear, even hatred of weakness in our selves, our leaders, our God. We tend to dismiss the powerless.

"Yet the foolishness of God is wiser than our wisdom," Paul writes, "and the weakness of God is stronger than our power" (1 Corinthians 1:25). One of the current questions with which thinking Christians of today wrestle: How can God be all powerful and yet allow so much human and natural disaster? What is God's will?

God's will. A final piece of rubbish for our compost heap is a misunderstanding of God's holy will. Each day we pray: "Your will be done on earth as it is in heaven." How then did we end up with words that are presumed to be consoling when a person is in pain, in grief, in agony: "It is God's holy will"? Pain and disaster are not God's will. There is no grief and agony in heaven, so how can God's will be for suffering on earth? "Your will be done on earth as it is in heaven."

Listen to God speak good news through Jeremiah, a prophet usually noted for his gloom-and-doom messages to a people beset by war and evil kings: "My plans for you are plans of peace (*shalom*) and not disaster... I have reserved for you a future full of hope" (Jeremiah 29:11-12).

If we want to believe that good news, then we will need to change our understanding of power. God sent Jesus in part to overturn what our society judges as important and powerful. God's understanding and exercise of power is evidenced in Jesus' overturning "how the rulers of this world lord it over their subjects" (Luke 22:25). Jesus puts flesh on the power of God when he removes his outer garment, takes a bowl of water, kneels in front of each of his friends, and washes their dirty, smelly feet (John 13:4-14). In a patriarchal society, power means control, management, getting one's way. For Jesus, however, power means relationship, attention, service and love.

How can God allow pain and evil if God is all powerful? God does not "allow" it. God has created us free, and we freely at times wreak evil on each other. God hates this evil and rages at it. God's will is not that Jesus be tortured to death. God hates betrayal, abandonment, scourging, mocking, false witness, abuse of power, death of the innocent Jesus. The crucifixion is not God's will, and only a sadist-god would "allow" it.

Rather, God is demonstrating a different kind of power. God is with, stays with, holds, supports, understands, cries with. If, as our many statues of the Pieta witness, Mary weeps over the broken body of Jesus, how much more God sobs. Those people who stay faithfully with us, listening, affirming rather than talking us out of our feelings, indeed even sharing our feelings of pain and distress and despair, these are the ones who have the most power in our lives. If human beings can offer such steady love to one another, how much more God! This is God's power: Emmanuel, God-with-us. This is God's will: to be with us, however we are, at every step in our aging process, to bring us *shalom* (Jeremiah 29:11). God's plans are plans of *shalom*, a Hebrew word meaning peace, and also health, wholeness and integrity.

To explore a new appreciation for God's will as peace,

shalom, we will need to reexamine not only power but pain, freedom and the full meaning of *shalom*. Power is ascribed to God constantly in our liturgies. So many of our formal prayers begin: "all-powerful" or "almighty" God. Twelve-step groups that help people recover from addictions refer to their Higher Power. Yet divine power is also associated with and longed for as rescue, fixing, magic, rather than with its meaning in Greek, "energy." The energy that heals the addict is not an almighty power out there somewhere, but the deep energy of God within the human heart and within the human community. Across cultures and centuries, the energy of life received heals and harmonizes. For example, the *Tao Te Ching* by China's ancient sage, Lao Tzu, describes a life process, a spirituality operating since the fifth century B.C.E., which taps into the divine energy in the universe.

Lao Tzu knows that all energy moves toward unity, but we Christians have our own way to understand God's power. We look to Jesus. If you want to see God, Jesus assures his apostle Philip the night before he dies, look at me (John 14:9). Jesus is a prophet strong in word and deed (Luke 24:19). We, however, have tended to equate his miracles with rescuing people from misery. On the other hand, theologians note that other Jewish prophets like Elijah and Greek "divine men" could heal and even raise the dead. It may be more helpful to look at Jesus' "power" as love and energy flowing through him to restore health, wholeness and even life. We see Jesus using all his love and energy to war against suffering, injustice and pain. To know what God wills, we look at what Jesus wills. That is always *shalom*, peace.

And more than peace, *shalom* also means wholeness, health and integrity. God hates pain and sickness. God's passionate desire is to heal suffering and fight injustice. If we change the noun, God's will, to a verb, what God wants, or what God passionately desires, we can perhaps break out of that mindset that God "permits" suffering. Just as Jesus passionately desired healing and wholeness for the people he encountered, so does God.

A passive God who "allows" smacks of the god of the

Greek philosophers whose highest attribute of perfection is *apatheia*, "without passion" (note our word *apathy*). Our God is not apathetic. Our God passionately desires our *shalom* and our freedom. All the books of the Jewish Scriptures sing of God's action of freeing a people from slavery in Egypt. Exodus freedom is a theme of Jewish writings and liturgies even today. God passionately desired freedom for Jesus all through his life, even in Gethsemane and on Calvary. God also wanted the people around Jesus to be free: freedom for the disciples who betrayed, slept, ran away and denied; freedom for soldiers, Sanhedrin, high priest and Pilate. Jesus did not want crucifixion, God did not want his crucifixion, but both of them desired freedom, both for Jesus and for those who would abuse it. And God's will for us? God passionately desires our freedom. God wants to be with us, however we are, at every step in our aging process, to bring us peace, health, wholeness, *shalom*.

Just as our waste, gathered in a compost heap, becomes food for microorganisms and earthworms, so their waste becomes humus. Humus, the rich and fertile soil, provides us with food. The cycle continues. Decay and death bring life. Whether in a personal, cultural or religious compost heap, the Spirit's force, *dunamis*, is at work to bring from death the humus, the human being who is fully human and fully alive.

CHAPTER THREE

Sowing

G od has planted so much in us from our mothers' wombs, and from our baptism into Christ. The word *baptizo* in Greek means "to be plunged into." Christ is both soil and the seed.

Being Plunged Into Christ

We are plunged into Christ, rooted and planted in him, the very ground of our being and of all being, this risen, cosmic Christ. And he is the seed, the origin of the gifts that will bear fruit as we age: first, the Holy Spirit and every other gift and fruit of the Spirit; then, our communion of sisters and brothers in the Body of Christ; finally, the grace that is God's own life and wisdom.

For Reflection and Prayer

Reflect first on the meaning of baptism, what you learned as a child, how the meaning developed as your life in Christ deepened over the years. How did those changes of meaning happen? How do you feel about the multiple meanings of baptism?

Most of us learned as youngsters that baptism washed away the original sin that stained each human being. True enough, but so much more. For some of us it meant, too, that we were saved. True enough, but what has "being saved" come to mean as we have been growing? For some of us, it meant that we accepted Jesus as our savior. How has our knowing and loving Jesus as uniquely personal and communally expressed been developing?

If we have been exposed to good preaching and adult education classes, if we have pondered in our own times of prayer, perhaps when a friend was choosing baptism, or a grandchild being presented for christening, then our understanding of this initial identification with Christ has been enriched. The "original sin" of Adam and Eve has been overcome by God's raising Jesus from death, the punishment for sin. Christ Jesus is victor over death, and also the "fear of death which held so many all their lives in slavery" (Hebrews 2:15). In this act of God, the raising of Jesus, not only is the human race freed from fear—and especially the fear of death— but the whole of creation, already freed yet groaning in slavery (Romans 8:22) waits for the final salvation. If salvation once meant "getting to heaven"—a minimum at best—now we understand the Latin root of the word, *salus*, as health and wholeness. Our being saved means our becoming ever more healthy, even though our bodily strength and health may diminish as we age.

Our being saved means working toward the final task of being human, integration, as psychologist Erik Erikson names it; wholeness, as Scripture calls it. The Hebrew word *yesh*, the root word of *salvation*, means literally "being set free in the open." Salvation is about our becoming ever more free in this world, not just the next. *Yesh* is the root of Jesus' own name, Yeshua. To be saved, then, means letting Jesus save us and claim us here and now. Salvation has not just to do with the hereafter. The good news is that we receive salvation now, health and wholeness now, freedom "in Christ" now.

Jesus is, however, more than our personal savior. Jesus, made Lord and Christ when God raised him from the dead (Romans 1:4), is made leader of the whole universe, center of every heart whether or not a given person recognizes Christ at his or her core. Jesus died to gather into one new family all the scattered children of God (John 11:52), although many have not yet recognized their new roots in him. According to Matthew's Gospel (25:37-40), those many will be surprised at the last judgment. "When did we see you hungry or naked or homeless or sick or in prison?" they will ask. To love the least of one's brothers and sisters, whether they be Muslim or Buddhist, agnostic or atheist, is to love the Christ at the core of each person. To be baptized is to be plunged into a new family, God's family, where all are equal sisters and brothers. We speak of being "incorporated" into the Christian community. The root of *incorporation* is the Latin *corpus*, "body." We are plunged into the Body of Christ in whom all the universe and its peoples are gathered. That doctrine can have quite practical ramifications. Rea tells of how the meaning of baptism changed for her as she experienced for the first time the death of a loved one.

In 1973, Jane Ago, S.S.N.D., and I lived together in Boston while we both did graduate studies. Because I was too far from my Chicago home, I often spent not only holidays but some Sunday dinners with Jane's family. Her father, both legs amputated, could not be left alone, so I volunteered to sit with him, to listen to his stories, to share a glass of rye. At the same time, I was aware of a growing aversion to a fellow student, a priest who drove a fancy car to school while I rode the MTA. Little did I know that Jane would ask him to Sunday dinners when I wasn't invited, and that he, Arthur, also sat with Mr. Ago. Without our knowing it, both Arthur and I were bonding with this seventy-four-year-old man as a kind of adopted father.

During our second year of studies together, Mr. Ago became critically ill and was hospitalized, on a ventilator. After class I would walk a mile to visit him in the hospital, while Arthur drove his big car. One day Arthur invited me to ride with him. Hmmmm..., I thought. It became a routine. We both simply sat with Mr. Ago, since his stories were cut off by that ventilator. On December eighth, an S.S.N.D. feast, Jane and I had planned a party for our Sisters in the Boston area, but now with her father so ill we were about to call it off. "No," Arthur offered, "Let me go and sit with him tonight." A marvel. That night they took him off the ventilator for a few hours, and Mr. Ago was able to pour out his regrets and fears to Father Arthur. Jane and I were sitting amid the after-party clutter, staring silently at the dying embers in the fireplace, when Arthur came in.

"I had a good talk with your Dad tonight, Jane," he announced. "He was afraid he wasn't a good enough father to you and your brother," Arthur continued, "but I think I was able to convince him that he was a fine father. After all, we have proof. Look what a fine father he has been to Rea and me."

At that moment, I saw so clearly that I could barely breathe. Arthur and I had become, for all our mutual aversion, truly brother and sister because of our love for our adopted father. "And I, if I am lifted up, will draw all to myself," Jesus promised. The death of that man lifted on a cross did indeed gather into a new family all the scattered and divided children of God. God had already, decades ago, made Arthur and me brother and sister. On that December night the pending death of a man whose very death drew us together made the new family of Arthur, Jane and me real. Our "being one in Christ," fruit of our baptism, became a practical, tangible, felt doctrine to me.

Christ is the soil into which we are plunged in baptism. He is also the seed planted deep within our selves. In Jesus' parable of the sower and the seed (Mark 4:3-9), the farmer of Jesus' time scattered the seed randomly. In God's plan, however, nothing is lost. God knows just how to press each Christ-seed into the soft earth of our hearts.

For Reflection and Prayer

Now remember your own baptism, or stories you may have heard, if you were an infant. Any photos that you can review? A baptismal dress passed around in your family? The candle or Bible you may have received if you were an adult? It is worth the time to dig out these items to contemplate. The more our memories can be concrete, the deeper our remembering and renewing of the experience. Do you know the date of your baptism? If your memory fails you, celebrate your baptism the next time you receive Holy Communion. Christ is planted anew in you each time you receive communion. Even if participating in the Eucharist in person is no longer possible, contact your priest or minister to arrange for communion to be brought to you, a possibility in all the mainline Christian denominations. If Holy Communion is not possible, how could God refuse your heartfelt prayer that God press the Christ-seed deep into your heart? This very moment, ask God. Know it is a reality.

The Seed Is Christ

Our baptism may have been sixty or eighty or one hundred years ago. The seed has sprouted and grown, but we may not recognize it. The Christ-seed we asked for this very moment is hidden deep in our self. This Christ-self is the "hidden self" that has been growing strong (Ephesians 3:16). For example, Jesus grew in wisdom, age and grace. Christ continues to grow in us. He grows in wisdom and grace in us, too, as we age. "It is all God's work and not our accomplishment" (Ephesians 2:8). We did have the fullness of wisdom and grace when we were baptized, as did Jesus and Mary his mother at their birth. Our capacity, like theirs, for wisdom and grace, however, was infantile. Our wisdom at ten years of age was the wisdom of a ten-year-old; and so was Jesus'. Our fullness of grace at twenty was just as full as we could be; and so was Mary's.

In the opening of John's Gospel the author uses a particular preposition when he writes about how in Christ we receive "grace upon grace" (John 1:16). The Greek for "upon" means never-ending. And so we might translate that verse: "Out of his [Christ's] fullness we have all received, grace upon grace upon grace upon grace upon grace upon grace...." With every influx of grace, Christ's fullness within us, a new capacity for grace is carved out. Our hearts expand. We are full of grace at twenty and full of grace at eighty, and our hearts keep expanding with each choice we make to love: to love the dog, the roses, the cousin we never see, the spouse we see too much of, the blue sky, the needed rain, the grocery clerk, the mother who died sixty-seven years ago, the oncologist, the woman who drools, the man who can never seem to hear, the child that pesters, the teen who delivers the paper, our very own self on healthy days and painful days, in cranky moments and in bursts of laughter. Grace upon grace upon grace upon grace....

For Reflection and Prayer

Would you stop reading for a moment and "count your blessings"?
A blessing in Hebrew means the sharing of, the very exchange of life.
God exchanges all that God is with us. We say that grace is the life of
God, freely given to us. How has God shared God's own life in the
dog, the roses, the cousin, the rain, the child, the pain, the laughter?
How does each of these—and your own personal list of grace upon
grace upon grace—carry the fullness of God's life into yours?

Grace defined as God's own life could mislead us, first into thinking we can define grace. To define means to set limits on, to delude ourselves that the infinitely knowable mystery of grace can be captured in human words. Second, we may wrongly think of grace as a thing. Rather grace is a Person, not so much a static gift but a dynamic process. We may not then count our grace upon grace upon grace, may not even count our blessings, as if they were things, objects given. Instead we count on Grace, we count on the Blessing One. We trust.

Finally, the greatest gift that God has planted in us is the Spirit. We who are rooted and planted in Christ are growing up in the Spirit, Christ's way of existing within us. We know we do not have a full-grown human male living inside us, but the Spirit is the way the risen Christ can live and move and be within us. The Spirit is Christ, present and active among us. The Spirit is also the bond, the love, which holds us together, the life blood of Christ's Body.

When the Spirit is sown in us, so are all manner of gifts. Faith, hope and "the greatest of these is love." Fruits of the Spirit begin to grow. "Love, joy, peace, patience, kindness, goodness, faithfulness, gentleness and self-control," Paul names them (Galatians 5:22). And of course, freedom (Galatians 5:1). Fruits of the Spirit are not virtues, actions or even attitudes that we can practice. Fruits just grow. Fruits happen because we are planted in Christ and the Spirit is planted in us. We are watered and weeded, growing through a layer of fertilizer and pushing day by day toward the sun.

CHAPTER FOUR

Growing

M any Scripture passages assure us of the ongoing growth of Christ's life in our hidden selves. Paul writes that if God loves us so much that God has given us the Spirit poured into our hearts (Romans 5:5) and the beloved Son as well, then how much more God wants to lavish on us all that God has to give! (Romans 8:32). This gift is not given drop by drop; it is abundant, lavish life (John 10:10). We are not given just some gifts and graces, but all that God has to give—the whole divine self. Who can take it in? Who has the capacity to take in all of God's own self?

Perhaps that is what makes Jesus and Mary so special in our tradition. Perhaps they alone could allow God to lavish on them all that God has to give. Twice Luke's Gospel points out that Jesus grew in wisdom and grace even as he grew in age (Luke 2:40, 52). If that moving into God was a gradual growing in Jesus, so Mary, too, would have grown in wisdom and grace. They would be filled with the very fullness of God (Ephesians 3:19). Yet the capacity of the twelve-year-old Jesus to be wise is not so great as the depth of a thirty-year-old. If Mary grew into old age, she was always full of wisdom and grace, but her capacity as a seventy-year-old was so much deeper than her capacity as a forty-year-old.

In Wisdom

How do we grow in wisdom? How would Jesus and Mary have grown in wisdom? Most people respond that it is not just experience, but reflection on our human and religious experience that makes us wise and grows us into the mind of

God. Jesus took retreats to be alone, whether for a night, or some time with just his friends. Luke tells us three times that Mary "pondered all these things in her heart." How much Jesus must have learned a contemplative attitude from her. To preach about lilies and sparrows and fishnets Jesus would have had to experience how beautifully they were arrayed, how precious and full of God every creature was. He was busy growing in wisdom as he pondered these creatures, other human beings and his God in his heart. The more fully human he became, the more fully he shared in God's mind, God's truth, God's wisdom. To move into God was, for him, to move into permanent insecurity. Who could know what the next day might offer, or where the Spirit of God or the needs of the people might lead him? He was experiencing in his mind, heart, will, emotions, body all that it meant to be human, and was thus growing into a wise human being.

To move into God is to move into the dynamic life of God, which is grace. Jesus was growing in grace until the moment of his death. His human experiences, his willingness to let all of created reality into him, to form and transform him, made him fully human, fully alive. And then, in the surprise that was resurrection, in his risen life, everything is once again turned inside out. All creation exists in Christ, is formed and transformed in him. "O wondrous exchange," our former liturgy for New Year's Day proclaimed, "that God and human beings could be so intertwined." "May this mingling of the water and wine," we once prayed in ancient Latin. Our modern translation reads: "By the mystery of this water and wine, may we come to share in the divinity of Christ, who humbled himself to share in our humanity." Because of the Word's becoming flesh, we human beings, through the Holy Spirit and baptism, are in the process of becoming divine, as Saint Gregory Nazianzus teaches (*Catechism of the Catholic Church*, page 641).

Fully Human and Fully Alive

Jesus was growing day by day in grace, accepting all that God wanted to lavish on him, the fullness of God's own life. Saint Irenaeus wrote at the end of the second century A.D. that the glory of God is the human being fully human, fully alive. The more Jesus experienced all that it was to be fully human and fully alive, the more he was giving glory to God, the more he was the glory of God in the flesh. On the cross his human body could hold no more of God. It burst open, utterly filled with the glory of God, manifest to those who believe. In weakness, powerlessness and death, the body of Jesus was filled with the glory of God.

Scripture promises us that we all, like Jesus and Mary, will be filled with the fullness of God (Ephesians 3:19). Will be—or are? Who knows? It is our hidden self that is growing strong. The First Letter of John witnesses to an abundance of life now, and even more glory promised us in the future: We are already God's children and what we will become has yet to be revealed (1 John 3:2). What we will become is "more than we can ask or even imagine!" (Ephesians 3:20). Now, some of us have very powerful imaginations indeed. Yet, it is to be more than even we can imagine!

What if that lavishing is not just a promise of future glory but our ever-so-loved and lavished-upon condition right now? This is what God hopes for, what God passionately desires for us: that we will let God lavish on us all that God has to give. So many of us want to "do God's will." God's will is not pain and diminishment and abandonment. God's passionate desire is that we open to all that God is, God's grace, the fullness of Christ. God's passionate desire is that we become just what God created us: human. Not angelic, not divine, but human—human beings, growing ever more fully human, and ever more fully alive. Thus we give God glory—now.

Although "growing" here seems to be an active verb, it is God who makes our hidden selves grow strong. It is futile, and harmful, to try to measure our growth or our strength. Jesus told a strong parable against those who would measure their

37

merit, even under the guise of giving thanks that they are not like other human beings, "like this tax collector here" who stands far off and cannot even lift up his head as he begs God's mercy (Luke 18:9-14). Paul told of his own futile efforts to win God's approval: "...in keeping the Law I was perfect" (Philippians 3:6). Now, he writes, after his conversion, a conversion not from sin or to a new religion but from self-satisfaction at his spiritual progress, he considers such spiritual achievement as so much dung for the sake of knowing Christ Jesus (Philippians 3:6).

For Reflection and Prayer

Take a piece of paper (at least 8 1/2" by 11") and draw seven or eight large circles on it leading to the top left corner. In the top left draw a sunburst, labeled God. Now reflect on some of the major events of your growing in wisdom and/or grace and write a key word for each in what are your stepping stones to God. You can then fold the sheet and tuck it into your journal.

Scripture tells us that growth is usually imperceptible while it is happening. After we have planted, we read in Mark 4:27, we go to sleep and overnight the earth begins to sprout. So is God's work of growing us often imperceptible rather than obvious, bold and/or miraculous. God works in the ordinary. *The Desert Call*, a monastic quarterly, published these criteria for accepting poetry:

> We try to find poems that do not refer directly, self-consciously to God or to religious experience, but rather poems that evoke the depths of human experience which is always pregnant with God. Since God is not a separate being but Being itself, we look for poems that depict our response to Being, whom we meet in muck, manure, blood, sweat, wrestling, swimming, chasing dogs, mourning, dancing, etc. Thus, like the ancient Jews, we shy away from mentioning his [sic] name directly in poetry, for fear of separating it from the life that utters it. (Maitland, *Aging as Countercultural*, page 131)

Finding God in all things and pondering that revelation in the ordinary grows us in wisdom and grace.

PART TWO

A S WE WERE WRITING THIS BOOK, *we were delighted to learn that the United Nations declared 1999 the International Year of Older Persons. In doing so, they set forth some principles:*

- *preservation of the independence of the elderly;*

- *the right to participate fully in society;*

- *access to quality care and services;*

- *opportunities for self-fulfillment;*

- *the affirmation of the dignity older people possess as valued members of society.*

This vision, if made specific in the various cultures of our planet, could encourage the tending of the rich, fertile soil of our aging. God's own vision of shalom for each of us, and every family, community, nation and people of the world is the same—and more. For this purpose God has sent the sun and the rain, the fresh breezes and clean air to nurture us as we grow. These are, of course, metaphors for the sun of justice, the light of the world, Jesus, as well as for the living water welling up from deep within us (John 7:32), the breath of God, the Holy Spirit. The light of Christ, the water and fresh air of the Spirit have, of course, been attending to us and tending us all through our lives.

In Part Two, we will focus on our ongoing development into old age. While God is never finished calling us to conversion and transformation, always clearing and plowing, sowing and growing, deepening our life in Christ and his Body, many of the initial movements in what will become an abundant harvest have been begun in the first half of our life.

Carl Jung noticed in his practice of psychotherapy that there was no problem in the second half of human life that was not, ultimately, a spiritual problem. At one time we considered anyone past forty years of age as in the second half of life, but as life expectancy lengthens, no doubt past fifty years is our second half. As God has begun in our first half to prepare the field who we are (1 Corinthians 3:9), so in the first half of this book we have set the stage for some spiritual exercises that will continue and intensify in this second part.

CHAPTER FIVE

Mary, Our Pioneer as We Age

We call on Mary, the mother of Jesus, who most likely grew old, to pioneer for us our journey of aging. When we were young, many of us had a devotion to Mary, the mother of Jesus. She was the mother some of us longed for, or the mother who expanded our own mother's care. We may have imaged her as our grandmother. Mary was one to turn to during our adolescent tensions with either parent, someone who, as we grew less innocent, could be our refuge in times of turmoil and sin.

For Reflection and Prayer

What was your own experience of Mary, mother of Jesus, as you were growing up? What was Mary like? How did she relate with you? Did you have a special name for her? Did she have a special name for you? If these are fond memories, rest in the joy they bring. Resting with Mary is contemplation. If you have never had a relationship with Mary, question yourself now. Did you ever hear about her when you were growing up? Were you jealous of her special place with God? Did she seem too good, and maybe too plastic, to relate with? Are you willing to learn to know her, perhaps to take her off the pedestal you or Church teachings have constructed? Are you willing to meet a real, flesh-and-blood woman who lives now, as do all our many mothering figures, many relatives and friends, with God?

Sometimes the pictures in our homes, the holy cards, the descriptions of Mary offered by our parents, teachers or preachers portrayed a smiling young woman carrying the infant or young Jesus. A particularly lovely image is one of two-year-old Jesus, asleep, lying sprawled across his mother's lap. Others of us can vividly recall Michelangelo's *Pieta*. Serene marble, serene mother. Perhaps some of us, somewhere, caught a glimpse in the centuries of Western art of a mother whose face is ravaged by pain as she stands under the cross. A few of us may have come across an artist's vision of the risen Lord greeting his mother on the day of the Resurrection.

Fully Human

Lest Mary become "good old plastic Mary," riding on the dashboard of our cars, let us look again at the image of Mary as portrayed in the Gospels and in our own experiences of her. Our first assumption is that anything we can say about the humanity of Jesus, we can say about the humanity of Mary. She was a living, breathing and very human being. Like her son, she was continually growing in wisdom and grace as she was growing in age. She is like us in all things except sin. Her growing more fully human and more fully alive each moment of her life gave glory to God.

Many intriguing, but often inaccurate, stories about Mary have been spun from the imaginations of those who crafted our apocryphal gospels and other unofficial teachings. One such story is that Mary received from Gabriel a kind of blueprint of her life which she could take out and consult, giving her inside information on what was to happen next. This would leave Mary very little freedom, an essential piece in God's will, God's passionate desire for human beings. Instead of consulting her blueprint, Mary, like us, had to search inside her own heart for the wisdom to make her decisions; her life was in no way programmed.

Another strange teaching is that, in order to preserve Mary's virginity, her baby did not enter the world through her birth canal but popped, all washed and smiling, into his mother's arms. The doctrine of Mary's virginity is not meant to demean Mary's sexuality. Jesus, like us in all things, entered this world as we all do, through that narrow space. *Angostos*, the Greek word for narrow, choked-up space, is the root of our English words *anxiety* and *anguish*. It was painful for Jesus to be born, ejected into the world by his mother, who obviously had her own pain and anxiety before and during the process.

In our own aging process, we want Mary to accompany us with her wisdom and grace, gained through her long experience and reflection. We might begin by reexamining these stories, using our own experience of what it means to be human, to be a real woman, to be a mother, to be open to God. As a real woman, she knew pain, sweat, blood, tears, anger, the pull of sexuality, the melting with tenderness, the anxieties of mothering and the aches of aging.

We presume she grew old. She certainly was at least forty-two when Jesus was arrested and crucified. With the Twelve and the other disciples gathered in the upper room at Pentecost, she was gifted with grace and power for mission and ministry. We hope she didn't die soon after this, but rather that she could use her gifts to build up the new community. We will look now at what we know of Mary from the Gospels, looking at her through what we know of her human feelings and experiences. We will conclude by exploring her freedom, joy, peace, love, kindness—all the fruits of the Spirit operating in her.

Blood

Mary's blood is the silent clue to a wonderful act of God. In Matthew's Gospel, she has no message from an angel, no understanding of God's plan and action. Although not specified, the missing of her menstrual period was undoubtedly Mary's first inkling that she was with child. Like us, she notices the changes in her body and understands that something is awry. How will she tell her mother? Her father? Her fiancé? What must her confusion have been? Jewish girls at that time were engaged at eleven and a half years, to be married at twelve, the age of adulthood for Jews of that time.

Stoning was the punishment for adultery. A wronged man could have his unchaste betrothed or spouse stoned, drowned or burned to death. But Matthew notes that Joseph was a just man, and so he decided to divorce Mary quietly. No death sentence, no capital punishment, although the Law gave him that "right." "Justice" in both the Hebrew and Greek languages means holiness. Joseph is a holy man. Holy people do not exact revenge. Instead, they are so imbued with God's own holiness, God's own justice, that they have compassion on the weak and even the evildoer. What being "put away quietly" would have meant for Mary was a life at home with her parents. She would have had no possibility of another marriage, no possibility of children. When her father died, if she had no brothers, she would be considered a charity case in her small town. Just in time, Joseph hears an angel in his dream.

How Mary's lack of menstrual blood must have set her trembling, for she knew she had not had sex with any man. She could only trust that, even betrayed by her own body, her God could do great things in her. Like so many of us who also are betrayed by our bodies through disease, stroke, heart attack, she prays with us this very day that God will do great things in our bodies.

In Luke's Gospel, Mary herself hears the angel's explanation of the amazing thing that was happening to her. Her obedience was in no way blind or unthinking. Mary's obedience included her hearing, her intelligent questioning, her pondering and eventually her yes. Mary's obedience was a process, not just for a moment on Annunciation day, but throughout her life. Those nine missed menstrual periods were, in Luke's version, no cause for worry but for energy and joy. Trusting her husband, she journeyed with him to Bethlehem. There in a cave, a barn, an ice-cold shelter of some sort, she shed her fertile blood in bringing forth her baby: "When they were there, the time came for her to give birth to her child. She bore her first born son. She wrapped him in swaddling clothes and laid him in a manger, because there was no room for them at the inn" (Luke 1:6-7).

We can be sure that if Jesus and Mary are "like us in every way," (Hebrews 4:15), the infant didn't simply pop into his mother's arms. Many women readers will have endured birthing a child and many men will have shared vicariously their pain and their joy. Women who pray with those two brief verses comment how difficult it must have been, how frightening for this young couple who did not have benefit of doctor or midwife, mother or even nearby Elizabeth, light or warm water. They note that if only Joseph had worked with livestock instead of wood he might not have tensed and trembled as he held out his hands for the crowning, bloody baby head. The holy family shared the joy and pain issuing from Mary's blood. She must have gladly shed her blood to give her son life.

A new family was again formed through an issue of blood some thirty years later. As the events on Calvary unfolded, Jesus gave birth to the church, his new community of friends, born of water and blood flowing from his open side.

> Standing by the cross of Jesus were his mother and his mother's sister, Mary the wife of Clopas, and Mary of Magdala.... The soldiers came and broke the legs of the first and then of the other who was crucified with Jesus. But when they came to Jesus and saw that he was already dead, they did not break his legs. Rather one soldier thrust his lance into his side, and immediately blood and water flowed out. (John 19:25; 32-34)

As Joseph caught the newborn's bloody body pushing out from his young wife's body, on Calvary it was Mary who was filled not just with the tension and trembling of the unknown. Her anguish must have shrieked to God as she watched her son brutalized. Their blood mingled in a new covenant that established forever the "kin-dom" of God. Her son never had the chance to age, but how she must have aged that day, as helpless as we who watch our children and grandchildren brutalized by gangs, drugs, alcohol or materialism. Many elders voice the wish that they could suffer in the stead of their innocent grandbaby who suffers from disease or burns or abandonment. What depth of agony must Mary have experienced in those hours. What trust she must have needed to believe that life is born of and in blood.

Sweat

Sweat is our body's response to anxiety, fear and panic. If Mary did not receive God's blueprint for her life from Gabriel, then her life was as full of anxiety as any human being's. It is probably the first emotion we feel as we are shoved through the birth canal. How squeezed and pushed we feel as we burst upon the world, how narrow our vision, how choked our feelings in those first moments of life.

Just as Jesus' suffering was not merely confined to the last few hours of his life, so Mary's anguish was lifelong. Just as Jesus would only preach what he had himself experienced, and he preached continually: "Do not be afraid," so Mary would have had to experience fear in order that God could grow in her the gift of trust.

Chronologically, her anxiety marked her as a human baby during her own birth, during the moments as an infant when she couldn't locate her mother, as she separated from her parents to be socialized with her age group, and when she was about to leave home to become Joseph's wife. Perhaps her anxiety pitched to panic when she realized she was pregnant. Perhaps, despite her fears, she traveled with a caravan to visit her cousin Elizabeth (Luke 1:39-45). She traveled the same road a few months later with Joseph, only to find no warm shelter as her labor pains began. And sweat she must have during labor.

The religious teachers of Judaism considered shepherds to be unclean, that is, in a state of alienation from God. Imagine then how a group of unwashed and smelly, boisterous and supposedly "sinful" shepherds must have frightened the young mother as they burst through the darkness to shout to her their good news, heard from angels in the fields.

Forty days later, what would Simeon's promise that a sword would pierce her own heart have done to Mary's heart? What fear must have flowed through her? Twelve years later, with his bar mitzvah, Jesus technically became a Jewish man. He, like all young adults, seemed to need to separate from his family of origin. This is a time of turmoil in most human families. Luke puts the anxious words directly on Mary's lips.

> When Jesus was twelve years old his parents went to Jerusalem for the feast of Passover.... As they were returning, Jesus remained in Jerusalem, but his parents did not know it. Thinking that he was in the caravan, they journeyed for a day, and looked for him among their friends and relatives.
>
> Not finding him, they returned to Jerusalem to look for him. After three days they found him in the temple... His mother said to him: "Son, why have you done this to us? Your father and I have been searching for you with great anxiety...." (Luke 2:42-46, 48).

Fear is not the only source of our human sweat. Strong emotions of all sorts may cause us to redden, breathe shallowly and sweat. Another incident that may have caused Mary to sweat in anguish, confusion and even humiliation might have been the conflict with Jesus as recorded in Mark's Gospel. This is the only time Mark mentions Mary. Mary seems to be displaced by the new family, a community of equals, which Jesus was creating.

> When his relatives heard this [that he was not eating] they set out to seize him, for they said: He is out of his mind...His mother and his brothers arrived. Standing outside they sent word to him and called him. "Your mother and brothers and sisters are outside asking for you." But he said to them in reply: "Who are my mother and my brothers?" (Mark 3:21, 31-33)

These words will likely evoke a strong identification with Mary in anyone who has an adult child. Who among us has never disapproved of one or many attitudes, actions and/or omissions by a grown child or grandchild over whom we have absolutely no authority? Who has not worried that a child, newly moved away from home, is getting enough to eat and the right kinds of food? What mother or father has not been stung by an adult child's sharp words? Who of us has not misunderstood the younger generation, sometimes so badly that a long-term rift is created? Who has not wondered whether the next generation is out of its mind?

Scripture invites us to identify with God, with Jesus, with Mary and the other biblical characters. To share feelings with someone is a path to intimacy. Jesus and Mary share the same tensions and troubles as any human parent and adult child with a will of his/her own. Share your feelings with Mary.

For Reflection and Prayer

If you are a parent, grandparent, aunt or uncle, remember those in the next generation of your own family. Invite Mary to sit with you as you call each one's name. Ask her to mother each one in a way you feel powerless to do. Ask her to share her heart of compassion with you. Ask her to bring to your awareness any need for reconciliation with a younger family member, and to help you find the wisdom to begin the dialogue again.

Tears

The sword of sorrow must have hung heavy in Mary's heart all through her life, both with Jesus and after his ascension. If she is like us in all things, then there were moments, perhaps even days, when she cried and even sobbed. Once again, Scripture offers us an opportunity to share Mary's feelings and to let her help us carry our own sorrows.

> Simeon blessed them and said to Mary his mother: Behold, this child is destined for the rise and fall of many in Israel. He shall be a sign that will be contradicted. And you yourself a sword shall pierce, so that the thoughts of many hearts may be revealed. (Luke 2:34-35)

Was Mary present when Jesus died on Calvary? Only John's Gospel stations her there. Neither Matthew, Mark nor Luke say that she was with Jesus when he died. Some of us have lost loved ones when we could not be present—through war, accident, or illness. We can be comforted by the possibility of Mary's absence at Calvary. Our grief is not lessened, but we can be comforted by the thought that Mary understands.

Others of us have held our children's or grandchildren's dead bodies. We have wailed with Mary: "Who knows a sorrow like my sorrow?"

> Standing by the cross of Jesus were his mother and his mother's sister, Mary the wife of Clopas, and Mary of Magdala. When Jesus saw his mother and the disciple whom he loved standing there, he said to his mother: Woman, behold your son. Then he said to the disciple: There is your mother. And from that hour the disciple took her into his home. (John 19:25-27)

According to John, Jesus' death created the new family in which all of us, the disciples whom he loves today, are given Mary as our mother. What of Joseph? It is possible, even probable, that Joseph had died before Jesus left home. Mark's Gospel tells us that it was Mary who came to take Jesus home. The pain of losing a child to death is equaled for many people by the agony of losing a beloved spouse. These losses are compounded by the deaths of many friends as we and our contemporaries age. Think of the friends Mary lost—through death, through misunderstanding of her son, through later disruptions as she moved from the routine of a housewife to become a missionary.

For Reflection and Prayer

Invite Mary, just the age you are now, to sit and have a cup of tea with you, or to sit next to your bed where you can see her eyes; even if you are physically blind, ask to see her face in the depths of your imagination. Tell her about one of your losses, in as great detail as you can remember. Then listen in silence to see how she comforts you. You may hear a word, see a smile, feel a presence or a warmth in your body. If nothing seems to happen, ask her for her comfort, whether as mother or as friend. Be quiet once more. Another day, share another grief with her. Know how much she understands your tears. Perhaps she uses Jesus' own words: "Nothing is lost." Not one of your tears is forgotten.

Like Us in All Ways But Sin

Whatever is said of Jesus may be said of Mary. She is like us in all ways, tempted like us, but without sin. Our temptations may be mental, willful, imaginative, but many arise in our emotions. Emotions are never sinful in themselves, but are God's gifts to us, signals to us of what we really think and want. For example, anger is often a signal that someone has violated one of our personal boundaries. As Mary moved into old age, if some young disciple treated her like a helpless child, she was likely to feel anger. Her dignity as a full human person had been disrespected. What did she do with the feeling? Emotions can give us the motion we need to right a wrong. Mary need not have been violent or abusive in her anger, but she would have clearly communicated that she did not want to be thought of nor treated as an infant.

Mary is our pioneer, first born of many sisters, as Jesus is our pioneer. Whatever we go through as a human being, becoming ever more fully human, more fully alive, she has endured as well. Some folks question the belief that Jesus and Mary experienced everything that is human and have pioneered the way through life for us. For example, they say that Jesus never had to experience labor pains, that Mary wasn't physically tortured or martyred. But they experienced all the things that life brought their way, and they felt those things just as any human being would.

For Reflection and Prayer

Think of a joy or a sorrow or a problem from your past life, or just yesterday. Ask Mary if she ever experienced anything like that. Is it your arthritis acting up? Did she have arthritis? Is it the reunion with your grandchildren? Is it an interior call to forgive an old grudge? How did Mary find the grace to forgive her son's murderers? Ask her, and then listen in silence.

Mary grew in wisdom, age and grace. If we think that the doctrine of the Immaculate Conception means baby Mary was all-wise and knowing, we do a great disservice to the much more important doctrine of the Incarnation, which is that God so loved what is totally human enough to become one of us. Mary at age one had the wisdom of a one-year-old, and at twelve the wisdom of a twelve-year-old. She was growing in wisdom all her life, as we grow in wisdom all our lives.

Mary, the First Disciple

Mary grew in wisdom as we all do, through a deepening of discipleship. The word *disciple* comes from the Latin word for "learner," and Mary was a lifelong learner. She not only experienced everything human, but she reflected on her experience and learned from it. "Pondering all these things in her heart" is the way Luke phrases it in his Gospel. In her heart she let God teach her. She was an eager learner, a disciple of God, a learner from God's Spirit. We need not think of supernatural visions and voices. Mary learned as we all do: from living life fully, from finding God at work in our feelings, our work, our loves, and from putting what she learned into practice.

Mary grew in age. That seems obvious, so let us emphasize the verb *grew*. All of us age, but all of us do not necessarily grow as we age. Some of us grow intellectually. We develop our curiosity. We enjoy our studies, if not formally, then through reading and educational programs; we keep on developing our minds even into oldest age.

For Reflection and Prayer

The fact that you're reading this book probably indicates you are interested in learning. How would Mary have continued her intellectual development? Ask her.

We grow in our ability to love. Some of us may lag behind in that growth because we lacked models of loving when we were youngsters, or we may have been so badly crushed in a love relationship that we have shied away from becoming close to anyone else. Some of us may not know how, or are afraid, to reach out to another in kindness, so badly treated were we in childhood or in an abusive marriage. And some of us may resent that Mary had specially chosen parents, and a most holy husband.

For Reflection and Prayer

Tell Mary how you feel about growing and/or getting stuck in your trying to love. She will not judge you as small or mean-spirited. Share your experiences of growing in love with her. Or show her just where your growth in loving became stunted.

In order to be fully human, fully alive we also must grow into our feelings. Jewish culture promoted feeling, and so we find that Jesus, Mary and the Gospel characters are passionate people. When we are born we are unable to think and to will. Infants are all feeling: anger, love, hunger, fear, pleasure.

Gradually in Christian history, however, as we moved away from our Jewish roots and into the stoic atmosphere of the second century, we as a church began to moderate and eventually stifle feeling. In our own lives as well, our family, culture or church may have made some feelings taboo. To grow as fully human as Mary then, we can ask her to help us feel all our feelings. As we talk about them with her, we can begin to trust their power and helpfulness in our lives.

Mary grew in grace. The angel Gabriel addressed her as "full of grace." How much more capacity for grace she would have had at twenty-two, at thirty-two, at forty-two, at seventy-two. How would Mary have grown in grace? Is she like us in this and are we able to be like her, continually growing in grace? Indeed. Mary was not full of grace because of her physical motherhood. In Luke 11:27-28 when a woman from the crowd praised her for biological motherhood, Jesus corrected that woman: Mary was to be praised because she had heard, taken in, digested, was in union with the Word, with God, with the Spirit. Perhaps Mary is the firstborn of many sisters and brothers just because she was most fully open to taking in all that God wants to lavish on all of us. To be so open to all that God lavishes is to be totally united with God, with a growing capacity for God as the human person ages. This is not something that Mary or we can measure. Mary didn't sit around Nazareth taking her spiritual pulse, planning some long retreat or discipline to sharpen her spirituality. The ability to receive grace is God's free and abundant gift.

For Reflection and Prayer

Talk over with Mary God's passionate desire for you to be full of grace and to grow in your capacity to receive all that God is.

Mission and Ministry of Mary

Mary most likely didn't sit around Nazareth at all once she was filled with the Holy Spirit on Pentecost. Luke opened his Gospel with the fullness of the Spirit working in Mary's heart, and then opened his Acts of the Apostles with the fullness of the Spirit gifting her (and 119 others) for mission and ministry. At about age forty-two, Mary, who once brought forth the historical Jesus, now will labor with his friends, male and female, to bring forth the Body of Christ, the new Church community.

Although Mary was at the cross only in John's Gospel, it seems that she may have been close by in Jerusalem on that terrible Friday, according to Luke's Gospel. On Resurrection day, Luke recorded an experience that "the eleven and the rest of the company" had of the risen Lord. Because of the parallels with the Acts of the Apostles, 1:14-15, when one hundred and twenty are gathered in what seems to be the same upper room, we can presume that Mary was among the group when Jesus appeared according to the last chapter of Luke's Gospel (24:33, 45-49). The disciples on the way to Emmaus had just recognized the risen Christ. As they were telling the whole community of their experience, Jesus stood in their midst, ate some fish, taught them a new interpretation of Scripture and commissioned them—all of them.

They set out at once and returned to Jerusalem where they found gathered together the eleven and the rest of the company.... Then Jesus opened their minds to understand the Scriptures.... "Thus it is written that the Messiah would suffer and be raised from the dead on the third day, and that repentance and forgiveness of sins should be proclaimed in his name to all nations, beginning from Jerusalem. You are witnesses of these things. And behold, I send the Spirit of my Father upon you. Stay in the city until you are clothed with power from on high." (Luke 24:33-49)

According to Luke, whose whole Gospel portrays the compassion and forgiveness of God in the person, mission and ministry of Jesus, the companions of the risen Jesus will carry that good news to all nations. Mary was among that company, she who has always been loved as the refuge of sinners. She went forth then and still proclaims that we must repent and receive God's mercy. She was then, and still is clothed with power from on high, receiving all the necessary gifts for mission as did the Eleven on Pentecost.

All of them with one accord devoted themselves to prayer, together with the women and Mary, the mother of Jesus, and with his brothers. In those days Peter stood up among the community (the company of persons was in all about 120) and said.... (Acts 1:14-15)

Today, when our children have left home, or when we have retired from our primary work, we may search for ways to keep life meaningful. Just as Jesus left, Mary accepted new power and energy (*dunamis* means both "power" and "energy" in Greek) for mission. If Ms. Lillian Carter, mother of President Jimmy Carter, could win our respect for traveling abroad with the Peace Corps in her sixties, let us imagine Mary with a life of missionary travel ahead of her. If Dr. Albert Schweitzer could surrender his talent for playing the organ and his academic Scripture scholarship to journey as an older man to tend the sick poor in Africa, how much more Mary would be drawn to minister to the needy of her world. Let us imagine Mary as a woman on fire with the Spirit, eager and powerful to spread the Good News of God's forgiveness in Jesus.

For Reflection and Prayer

To whom was Mary sent? What was her message? How did her story deepen and intensify as she grew in wisdom and grace on mission? How did her process of aging help her on mission and how did it hinder her? Ask her.

If Mary is like us in all things except sin, then her aging slowed her down. Her brain had its "senior moments," its tangles, lapses of memory and confusions. Her joint pain may have made her snappish (even Jesus snapped a lot at his own friends). Imagine her getting up to face the day from a pallet of straw on the floor. No air conditioning, no central heating, no electric blanket to keep arthritic joints from freezing up overnight. Her dimming eyesight may have made her more dependent. ("Another will lead you," Jesus had warned Peter about his old age.) Her fading hearing may have made her feel gradually more and more cut off from conversation. There were for her no hearing aids, no cataract surgeries, no eyeglasses.

For Reflection and Prayer

Imagine Mary as an old woman, even older than you are now. What does she look like? Ask her what keeps her alive and alert, eager and full of power. Ask her to share her energy for the Good News with you. Listen.

The former general of the Jesuits, Pedro Arrupe, who was himself terribly debilitated in his old age, wrote this to his men, and to all of us. It is a message that undoubtedly Mary, in her old age and even debilitation, surely must have lived.

> Nothing is more practical than finding God, that is, than falling in love in a quite absolute, final way. What you are in love with, what seizes your imagination, will affect everything. It will decide what will get you out of bed in the morning, what you will do with your evenings, how you spend your weekends, what you read, who you know, what breaks your heart, and what amazes you with joy and gratitude. Fall in love, stay in love, and it will decide everything.

All gifts of the Spirit are for the building up of the community, the Body of Christ. "And the greatest of these is love!"

For Reflection and Prayer

With whom are you in love? What gifts of the Spirit do you experience? Which gifts might have been special for Mary? Ask her.

Before Saint Paul composed his "hymn to love" in 1 Corinthians 13, he listed some of the Spirit's gifts for ministry. Mary would have received any or all of the gifts that the twelve apostles did. How did she develop them? Read Paul's list below slowly, and ask her.

To each is given the manifestation of the Spirit for the common good. To one is given through the Spirit a word of wisdom and to another, a word of knowledge according to the same Spirit, to another the gift of faith by the same Spirit and yet to another the gifts (*charismata*) of healing by the one Spirit. One does works of power (*dunamis*), another speaks as a prophet, another is able to discern spirits, another receives all kinds of tongues and another the gift of interpreting tongues. (1 Corinthians 12:7-10)

For Reflection and Prayer

Consider your own life in dialogue with Mary. She is your age as you share a conversation about the gifts you might have in common. Ask her to help you remember some times when you spoke "a word of wisdom" and to let you imagine how she used her gift of wisdom in the young community. What special knowledge do you have which builds up the Body? What special knowledge might she have had? Speak to Mary about your faith and your doubts, and listen as she speaks about her own when she was your age. Remember, she is like us in all things. When have you been a healing force—in your circle of family, friends, coworkers, church? When was Mary? Mary was surely gifted with prophecy. She did not see the future or make predictions, but like all New Testament prophets she was so close to the mind and heart of God that she dared to speak a word of comfort or a word of challenge in her community. When in your life did you speak in God's name? What other gifts might the two of you have which are not listed by Paul?

So many gifts of the Spirit that build up the community are much more ordinary than those mentioned by Paul. Remember any community in which you participate—your family, neighborhood, VFW, leisure club, class reunion committee, state government, local branch of Pax Christi—and the gifts you bring to it. Humor? Patience? An ability to notice details? A willingness to do the scut work? Planning or cleaning up? A pleasant voice to solicit volunteers by phone? Mediating and reconciling? Prayer, not just leading it but praying between gatherings? Love?

Later in his own life, writing his last letter, Paul penned another list of spiritual gifts:

> Having gifts which differ according to the grace given to us, let us use them. If the gift of prophecy, in proportion to our faith; if ministering, in our serving. If we have the gift of teaching, let us teach; if we exhort, in exhorting. Let the one who gives, give generously and the one who leads, lead with a sense of responsibility. Let those who show mercy, do so with cheerfulness. (Romans 12:6-8)

Just as prophecy in the early Church had nothing to do with future predictions, so ministering was not the responsibility of the ordained, for there were no ordained as yet. Baptism gives us all gifts of ministry, a Greek word, *diakonia*, which simply means serving. It is an aspect of love, another name for the Holy Spirit who is poured into our hearts with baptism (Romans 5:5).

For Reflection and Prayer

With Mary as your dialogue partner, go back over each decade of your life. How did you serve during the first ten years of your life? How did Mary? How did you serve during your teenage years? How did Mary? How did you serve in your twenties? How did Mary? And so forth.... How did the quality of your service change? Whom have you taught? How did you teach? Whom have you exhorted? To whom have you given and not counted the cost? Whom have you led? Review with Mary your sense of responsibility. How did it develop? When were you overly responsible? When did you shirk responsibility? She is gifted with mercy to reassure you. How are you gifted with mercy? Try to remember in as much specific detail as you can times when you offered mercy and compassion.

Mary in Ministry to Us

Mary is like us in all things. Even in her youth, she was preparing to age well by accepting, perhaps with questions and struggle as we watch her with Gabriel, God's passionate desire for her: that she receive all that God wanted to lavish on her, all that God is. And yet her life was the same mix and rhythm of joy and sorrow, pain and pleasure, as our own. Whether we are parent or spouse or friend, we know the humdrum and the crises of living a daily life, ever more fully human, ever more fully alive. If she is truly human, then we can remember, without shock, that Mary was an unwed mother, mother of an imprisoned man, a condemned man and executed criminal; that Mary was grief-stricken by death—Joseph, her own parents, her son; that Mary was a woman falsely accused, homeless, a refugee. She was a woman like all women, marginalized by patriarchy, oppressed by her religion, but the first disciple, the woman at Jesus' first supper. Mary was a woman daily growing in wisdom, age and grace, fired by the Spirit, gifted for ministry, powerful in mission, centered in God. She was an aging woman, an elderly woman, an old woman.

For Reflection and Prayer

Let us pray the song that Luke put on the young Mary's lips, transposing it in our imaginations to her song of later years, of aged years.

My heart proclaims your greatness, O my God,
and my spirit rejoices in you, God, my savior!
For you have looked on me and blessed me,

poor, and a serving woman.
From this day all generations will call me blessed,
for you have done great things for me.
Holy is your name! Your unconditional love lasts from
    age to age.
You show strength with your arm, scattering the proud
and lifting up the powerless.
You fill the hungry with every good thing
and send the rich away empty.
You remember your kindness and your faithfulness
    to your people,
as once you promised Abraham and Sarah,
kindness to their children forever. (Luke 1:46-55)

For Reflection and Prayer

*Now pray this canticle as your own. In place of "Abraham and
Sarah," insert the names of your parents. Then reflect: What in this
contemplation of Mary has affirmed your love for her and your faith
in her son? What has stretched you and challenged you? What more
do you want to know? Ask her. And keep on searching.*

CHAPTER SIX

Being Tended

A s we age, we may experience not only the comfort of the gentle rains and breezes of the Spirit, but the slashing torrents of storms that break branches and scatter fruits. We may not only receive the sweet sunshine of Christ, but we may become parched and need pruning as we age. We may need another round of fertilizing. As Paul writes: "...only God gives the growth. The one who plants and the one who waters have a common purpose...and we, we are God's field" (1 Corinthians 3:7, 9).

What we suffer will strengthen our roots. Rooted and planted as we are in Christ, in God the ground of our being, we cannot be uprooted. No matter how old we are, we can be transformed and conformed to Christ. And in the end we will be harvested by our gardening God.

Watering the Earth

Water is a source and symbol of life. It is the most predominant part of our physical being. Without water there can be no life, but paradoxically water can also destroy. Too much water kills. Gentle and sustained watering brings life and growth. Saint Irenaeus, bishop of Lyon, wrote about the value of water about A.D. 180:

> Just as dry wheat cannot be shaped into a cohesive lump of dough or a loaf held together without moisture, so in the same way we many could not become one...without the water that comes from heaven. As dry earth bears no fruit unless it receives moisture, so we also were originally dry wood and could never have borne the fruit of life

without the rain freely given from above....[We] have
received it through the Spirit. (Johnson, *Friends of God and
Prophets*, page 59)

So much, both simple and profound, has "watered" us in our
lives—relationships, attitudes, behaviors (expressed or
received), stances toward life that have nurtured growth. As
one of our octogenarian respondents reminds us—"Old age is
not a dead end, if it is a real relationship with God." Even if
many of the people who have "watered" us in life are taken
from us in our old age, God always remains faithful and
continues to invite us: "All you who are thirsty, come to the
water!" (Isaiah 55:1). Jesus adds to that invitation the promise:
"Rivers of living water will flow from within" (John 4:38).

How God 'Waters' Us

Watered earth has a rich aroma. Our soil has been plowed and
aerated, its clods broken apart so that the water can soak each
particle of earth. What a smell to savor. And how many
memories, rich and deep, to savor. One of our eighty-year-old
respondents shared the following story which illustrates how
"pondering in our hearts" even some of the most simple
memories can become a plentiful watering, inviting a rich
savoring of the ways in which our good God tends us.

> When I was a child one night there was a fierce thunder
> and lightning storm, a bit out of the ordinary. A clap of
> thunder scared me and I called to my Dad. He rushed
> upstairs to comfort me. As he put his arms around me, he
> said, "Little girl"—his pet name for me—"nothing is going
> to happen to you because God loves you." With his arms
> around me I fell asleep. You know, often as I sit in a chair I
> think of those arms, God's arms, and I just experience
> peace and quiet. I think of what our Lord said, "Suffer the
> little children" and even at eighty, that is a quality I desire
> in my life.

This woman does not need to use words to respond to God's
presence, the sensation of God's arms around her. As Saint

Thérèse of Lisieux responded when asked what she said to Jesus: "I don't say anything. I love him." We, too, can remember God's love and respond with a wordless love. Often during each day, without formulating a prayer, we remember and love various people, pets and other creatures. This is a way of "praying always," as Saint Paul urged. Instead of having to make up a special prayer for each happy memory that floats through our minds, our feeling of warmth, gratitude and love is a prayer without words.

For Reflection and Prayer

Take time to reflect upon how your relationship with God has watered the soil of your life in the past. How has your life with God developed over the years? Changed? Become more real and honest? What relationships, whether human, or with any part of creation such as pets, flowers, trees, ocean have helped you to grow and flourish? List them in your journal. Or find some photos to paste in your journal. Contemplate these creatures as you cut and paste so that you may find, as Gerard Manley Hopkins writes, the "dearest freshness deep down things" in each one.

While in other parts of this book we remember some of life's painful moments, in this chapter the focus is on the more joyful moments, moments that once caught our attention and became vehicles for God's tending us.

For Reflection and Prayer

List any relationship in which you experienced being the "twinkle in the other's eye"—mother, father, brother, sister, cousin, spouse, daughter, son, grandchild, friend, colleague, teacher, student, even pet.

Most relationships (with the possible exception of a dog!) have their up and down moments. As we gather specific memories of some of those human persons who have nourished us, we may notice that these persons reflected attitudes or demonstrated behaviors that become easier to appreciate and imitate as we grow older and develop a greater capacity for gratitude.

Gratitude is the first attitude we will explore, and then hope, humor, wonder, simplicity.

One of the most frequently cited gifts of aging is an increased capacity for gratitude. The Psalms give frequent voice to gratitude:

> I thank you, God, with all my heart;
> I recite your marvels one by one,
> I rejoice and exult in you!
> I sing praise to your name, Most High. (Psalm 9:1)

Gratitude oftentimes rushes without words as we notice the most simple elements of everyday life: the surprises of nature, the beauty of a Mozart concerto or the song of a bird, a note or visit from a friend, the flash of color as a hummingbird or finch darts past our window. Slowing down physically at this time of life allows us to notice, a simple definition of contemplation. To contemplate, to notice and be absorbed in God's creatures, leads us to be grateful. As some of the frenzied rushing around of earlier years abates and there is the time to notice, to savor, to be grateful, we may be praying without words. Just the heartthrob of gratitude is itself a prayer of gratitude. Prayer can thus fill our day, as we notice and follow our grateful hearts as they leap wordlessly to the Creator.

For Reflection and Prayer

In your journal, create your own litany of gratitude. See if each day you can find five things for which you are grateful and list them. Some members of Alcoholics Anonymous find fifty items each day! A litany of gratitude for the members of your family might be used in your funeral liturgy. To create such a litany may well be a graced time not only of grateful remembering of very specific gifts received from your family, but also of re-membering, a time to pray for reconciliation among all of you.

Another attitude that can flourish as we age is hope. In his journal, later published as *Markings*, former secretary general of the United Nations, Dag Hammerskjöld wrote how he often struggled with despair. In it he also often recorded the words from a hymn his mother read to him each New Year's Eve: "The night approaches now ____." Eight years before his death, however, he responded to these lyrics quite differently. He began with "The night approaches now—" but he continued on with a new and now well-known vision: "For all that has been—thanks! for all that shall be—yes!" "Hope, which sustained him for the rest of his life, had been born," comments David Maitland (*Aging as Countercultural*, page 97). Hammerskjöld had accepted his one and only life with gratitude and looked forward to the future, not with optimism, but with a willing hope. He could, as the First Letter of Peter urges us: "Be ready to give an account of the hope which is in you" (1 Peter 3:15).

For Reflection and Prayer

Let us pray with the psalmist:

> I believe that I shall see the goodness of our God
> In the land of the living.
> Put your hope in God. Be strong, may your heart be bold.
> Put your hope in God. (Psalm 27:13-14)

Humor is another robust gift of aging. In older age it takes on a new capacity for healing. "Those who laugh...last" a bumper sticker reminds us. Some of us have a better developed sense of humor than others. One day one of our respondents asked her Dad, well into his nineties: "What does being old mean to you?" He chuckled and retorted: "It's like sitting on a volcano—you don't know when it's going to erupt." Another day she asked him how he felt, he replied, "Much better than yesterday." She said, "Why did you say you felt good yesterday?" He quickly replied, "Because I didn't know how well I was going to feel today."

Some cartoon strips are portraying a more realistic view of older age. In 1998, the Canadian strip "For Better or Worse" treated the death of the grandmother and the trials of the grandfather who is trying to cope. "Family Circus" frequently portrays the children in contact with their dead Grandpa who watches over them from heaven. Single cartoons make a quick point. Two of our favorites: in "Frank and Ernest," we see the two characters as old men on a park bench. One says "I may be over the hill, but I took the scenic route to get here!" Our second: a small but upright elderly woman glaring into the face of Night Nurse. She wags a finger, saying: "Young woman, I have lived through the Depression, three wars and numerous police actions, have taught for 50 years, balanced a budget of hundreds of thousands of dollars, was principal of schools with over a thousand children, and you are telling me when to go to bed?"

May Sarton has journaled about the attitude of wonder to be recultivated in older age:

> Growing old.... What is the opposite of "growing"? "Withering" perhaps? It is, I assume, quite easy to wither into old age, and hard to grow into it.... And maybe growing old is accepting regression as part of the whole mysterious process. The child in the old person is a precious part of his being able to accept the slow imprisonment. As he is able to do less, he enjoys everything in the present, with a childlike enjoyment. (*House by the Sea*, page 27)

The child in us can reconnect with the children in our lives. With joy and wonder we may have marveled at the good chemistry that often exists between elders and small children. Grandparents are able to play with and enjoy grandchildren in a special way, and not just because they go home! As an imaginative three-year-old grandchild invites us to join her in acting out all the songs and roles in *The Sound of Music* we may find ourselves drawn spontaneously into her world of imagination and wonder. Our inner elder and our inner child meet and delight in these encounters. One woman tells of her granddaughter, Lauren, coming to grips with some of the mysteries of the universe—God, life, death—at the age of three.

Lauren noticed a leash hanging on the rack at her grandmother's and inquired, "Nannie, I didn't know you had a doggie." Her grandmother explained that they used to have a dog, but she had died. "Oh, you mean she's in heaven with my grandpa and God, Nannie." "That's right, Lauren." "But Nannie" she persisted a little more forcefully, "Why do you still have her leash?" Her grandmother explained about wanting to keep a reminder of the dog. "But Nannie," this time really puzzled, "What if God wants to take her for a fly?"

Another day when a trip to Friendly's Restaurant for ice cream coincided with a particularly spectacular sunset, Lauren wanted to know who made the sunset. Her grandparents told her that God did. A few days later when she was visiting their home she urgently summoned them outside. "Nannie, Grampie, come quick. God's making another Friendly's sunset for us."

Somehow in the busyness of adult life our childhood sense of wonder and awe often is squelched by many demands and responsibilities. As we age one of the attitudes that nourishes us abundantly is a reclaiming of this stance of wonder at the mysteries and beauty of our world.

Another attitude that can sustain us as we grow older is simplicity. Some of the layers of needing approval and feeling driven to meet others' expectations fall away. Sometimes, willingly or unwillingly, we let go of things and possessions which have meant much to us. Or they are painfully stripped away. Simplicity can be embraced or forced upon us. We probably experience elements of both. Embracing simplicity has ramifications far beyond our one and only life. We know that our only hope for survival as a global and ecological community is to be able to learn to live more simply and gratefully.

For Reflection and Prayer

What attitudes do you want to cultivate in order to nourish yourself and your community as you move into your elder years? Take some time today to "practice" wonder. Take a long, loving look at someone, something in your world today. What do you experience?

In the next chapter we will reflect on some of the behaviors toward self and others that foster wellness, a healthy and grace-filled aging. In this section as we reflect on the watering of our soil, being tended, we highlight two behaviors that are critical as we age—active listening and encouraging. They are elements of being tended because through these behaviors we share in God's own tending of us. God is first the active listener to our hearts, God is first our encourager.

Our capacity for hearing may not be as acute as in our early decades, but our capacity for active listening is a kind of hearing that can become more refined and accurate as we grow older. Active listening invites us to focus fully on what the other person is saying—not only their words but also their body language and feelings. It requires us to set aside our own internal "noise"—judgments, assumptions, preoccupations. It asks us to suspend mental preparations for rebuttal, response, and to attend as fully as possible to what we are being told. It invites us to enter as fully as we are able the "holy ground" of another's experience.

For Reflection and Prayer

Take time now to remember an experience when you felt fully heard. What was that like? Who are/were the person/persons? What do you remember most about this experience?

Sometimes when we listen, we think the other expects our advice. In active listening, however, it is not advice but the response, often an understanding silence or touch of the hand, that empowers the other. In times of conflict, instead of a quick-tongued argument, a moment of silence after each one speaks can allow the other to be really heard, her/his words absorbed and better understood. In being understood comes our freedom to explore and to experience our own internal but sometimes imprisoned wisdom.

The word *encourage* has its roots in the notion of "giving heart to." There is much in the world—personal, social, global—that can cause us all to lose heart. One of the gifts that we can give to our younger friends and family as well as to each other is the gift of encouragement.

This is not a Pollyannaish, unrealistic optimism that can turn people off with its artificially cheerful ring. Instead, the act of encouraging is discovering the positive, being generous in noticing and affirming the positive in the other. It is quietly standing by another during those times when he or she has lost heart for whatever reason.

For Reflection and Prayer

Who has tended you with encouragement? When? How? Try to be as specific as you can as you ponder this joyful mystery in your life.

Sunshine

What will nourish us now is the sunshine that sweetens us, the Light to whom we tend. Even if we have never seen a farm or planted a garden ourselves, we have seen plants stretch toward the sun. If you have never noticed even that, then find an indoor plant, or ask for one, and set it in the sunshine in your room. After a few days, you will see how its leaves turn to the light. And we do now, turn to the Light.

We will tend to ourselves, tend to our relationships, tend to the earth. Of course we will do this because it is the Spirit who tends us. We will do it in the company of Mary and with the guidance of Saint Paul. It is the Spirit who leads us and turns us to the Light. We tend to the Spirit in response. "We do not know how to pray as we should but the Spirit deep within us prays continually, putting our inarticulate groans into words which God can understand" (Romans 8:26).

One of the sadnesses of older age is that we thought then we would have the time and take the time to pray. Now we sit in our comfy chair, perhaps looking out the window at some greenery or drifting snow, and keep dozing off. Or we are housebound, can no longer get to church and have such little stimulation that we can hardly rouse ourselves to pray at home. Or we are flat in bed, in pain, and cannot pray. The good news about prayer, Paul teaches us in the passage from Romans, is that prayer is not our work, but the Spirit's work within us. The

Spirit prays continually, "joining our spirit to God's"—whether
we are awake or asleep, medicated for pain or alert, in full
possession of our minds or in the beginning stages of
wandering off. The Spirit deep within us who knows our
depths and the depths of God (1 Corinthians 2:10-11) joins us to
God at that deepest level. The Spirit within us (Romans 8:15-16)
keeps calling out God's name, whether we can attend to that
call or not. The name for God that Paul heard in his heart is
"Abba"; for Saint Augustine, God was "Beauty, ever ancient,
ever new." Julian of Norwich imaged Jesus as "our mother,
endlessly carrying us in his womb." Saint Francis de Sales
wrote of Jesus: "Be at peace; and let your weary, listless heart
rest against the sacred loving breast of this Savior who, by his
providence is a father to his children, and by his gentle, tender
love is a mother to them."

For Reflection and Prayer

*What might Mary have called God? How might she have imaged God?
What name does the Spirit call God deep within your heart? If you are
not sure what the Spirit names God in your deepest self, sit in silence
for a while and see what you can hear.*

Praying Always

Unless you have your radio on, you are not aware of the swell
of voices and music filling your room as you read in what
seems like silence. Yet the radio waves permeate your space. So
does the Spirit. Our prayer is like a tuning in of our radio,
catching the cry of the Spirit deep within us. The Spirit puts our
inarticulate groans into words that God understands. Some
feelings and fears are too deep for words. The Spirit knows that
even if we cannot speak them, God catches the cry of the Spirit.

Sometimes we do speak in our prayer. Whether we pour
out our hearts to God as the psalmists, Jesus, Mary and Paul
did, or whether we use formal words of prayer, we are still
subject to the prayer of the Spirit, which reaches the depths of
us, and the depths of God. The Spirit who sets free reminds us,

too, just how free God is. God will not perform on demand, or even necessarily show up in our times of formal prayer.

For example, an eighty-two-year-old who is a hospice volunteer found a spiritual director because, she complained, every time she tried to pray in church, at a worship service, or in her daily early morning quiet time, she would fall asleep. Why was she, who valued prayer all her life, ending her days without a robust spiritual life? What had she done wrong? Was there any hope?

Her director, instead of focusing on her discouraging attempts at formal prayer, asked about her relationship with God. "We're fine together," she smiled. "God goes with me as I do my home-visiting. I surely couldn't say such wise words to my patients and their families if God were not in my heart and on my lips." The director marveled. This woman had begun, after her retirement from teaching, to be a hospice volunteer, traveling alone through a rural county in heat and snow, to comfort the dying. Yet through it all she was not alone. God and she were companions, co-ministers, friends. Without knowing it, the volunteer's "God-talk" was so integrated in her life that she was even paraphrasing Scripture—"in my heart and on my lips"—to describe her openness to God. This hospice volunteer and her director have met once a month now for two years. It is still difficult for the volunteer not to perform well during prayer time. Yet she must admit: "God is filling everything all day long. Except my daily time for prayer!"

Some may discount their just sitting or lying with relatively empty minds. Yet they come away from such periods feeling rested, often more centered. They have not been conscious of praying, and have not used any words. This kind of resting is, for those of us rooted and planted in Christ, a kind of contemplation. Contemplation of a human being, the stroking of a pet, a deep and fresh look at a photo or an artistic reproduction, listening to a favorite piece of orchestral music, watching the waving of a tree's branches, savoring a glass of orange juice, all of these are ways to contemplate. The whole of creation reveals and communicates God to those who have eyes to see, ears to hear, hearts open to beauty.

"The world is charged with the grandeur of God," writes Gerard Manley Hopkins. To watch, hear, notice, savor is to enter more deeply into that speck of God's creation, and even without being able to articulate it, there we may well discover God.

Body and Emotions In and As Prayer

We learn from the Scriptures that we can use more than our minds and wills to pray. We are invited to pray with our whole selves: mind, will, bodies, emotions, imagination and memory. The psalmists urged us to clap our hands in prayer, and more than likely we have clapped our hands spontaneously in delight or wonder or happy surprise. We may not have formulated the words: "I thank you, God, for_____," but is that not exactly what our clapping meant? We may have dug our toes into the warm sand at the beach and smiled inside, no words, just a feeling of well-being. Some seniors deliberately use their bodies to pray, to stay flexible by moving in prayer to a piece by Mozart on the radio, a familiar hymn sung while dancing, or a modern hymn played on a tape or CD. Perhaps you have seen seniors in public parks moving slowly and deliberately, alone or in a group. They may well be practicing the Chinese form of bodily meditation, Tai Chi, which loosens our deepest interior energy while keeping us aware of our bodies.

Feeling our emotions is an excellent way to pray, and is found on about every page of Scripture. Are we afraid? Pray. Are we angry? Pray. Are we sorrowing? Pray. Are we in love? Pray. The psalms are loaded with emotions of every sort. The composers of these songs and poems wanted to show God just how they were feeling.

For Reflection and Prayer

If you have a Bible, check out the following psalms when you feel a particular feeling. Do not merely read the psalm text. Pray it. Offer your feelings to God.

Laments in sadness: Psalms 22, 32, 43, 51, 71, 80
Praise in glad times: Psalms 48, 104, 117, 135, 150
Curses in angry times: Psalms 35, 59, 69, 109, 137, 140

What does it mean to pray our emotions? First we feel them, without judging them as right or wrong, bad or good. They come from within us and we are good, so—as Jesus says—don't be afraid. Emotions just are, and we bring them to God, sometimes with words like the psalmists, sometimes without words.

For example, one woman returned from vacation with her sister to report that she hadn't prayed all the time she was away. "Oh," commented her spiritual director, "what did you do?" "We went for long walks every day in the woods behind her home." "Were you having conversations on these walks?" "A little, but not much. Both of us were just enjoying the coming of spring back there. The birds are back, you know, and were singing. The sun was warm on us because the trees are at that lacy stage." "And you were feeling...?" "I was feeling warmed and happy and peaceful and in a kind of gentle awe at how much I loved the birds and lacy trees and my sister. Yes, (she was surprising herself), how much I loved my sister." "Now image Jesus looking at you as you walk along, feeling all those feelings, noticing all that beauty. How is Jesus?" "Why (she was surprising herself again), he is feeling warm and happy and in love with me, and my sister." "Would he feel that way toward you every day on your walks? Wouldn't he expect you to go to church?" the director teased. "I think I was in 'church.' Although I didn't say any words of thanks or love, I was feeling it. I wasn't worried about anything, but I was just there, in the beauty and the warmth."

Imagination in and as Prayer

We are also encouraged to use our imaginations to pray. Saint Ignatius Loyola, founder of the Jesuits, offered a kind of contemplation that calls on our imaginations. We want to see the scene in technicolor, hear the soundtrack in our mind, smell the smells, taste the tastes, feel the temperature and textures and the clothing on our skin. Ignatius invites us to join Jesus in a Gospel scene. Let's do it now in a way that stirs both our imaginations and our memories. We will use two Gospel scenes, one of the four friends who bring the paralytic to Jesus, removing the tiles of the roof in order to lower the paralyzed man in front of Jesus (Mark 2:1-12). The second will be a paraphrase of the raising of Lazarus (John 11:1-45).

Jesus deals with paralysis (based on Mark 2:1-12). While Jesus was teaching in his own home in Capernaum, there was no way for four men carrying a stretcher with their paralyzed friend on it to break through the crowd that filled the house and thronged so thickly around it. Three of them climb to the roof of the home and remove pieces of it, creating a hole large enough to lower the stretcher. Imagine the amazement of the folks around the house as the four struggle to hoist the pallet and the man to the roof. Imagine the surprise of the crowd in the house as they watch this stretcher swing back and forth as it is carefully lowered before the eyes and feet of Jesus.

You are that paralyzed person. Remember some painful incidents, some harsh words that paralyzed you in the past, or even just last week. You might remember years or even decades of feeling paralyzed. When have you felt tightly bound, emotionally frozen, spiritually paralyzed? Now remember four friends, relatives, loved ones who did, would or could bring you to Jesus. Image these four struggling to lift you to the rooftop. What feelings arise in you as the pallet on which you are lying so helpless swings up to the roof, and then down again? How is your trust? In your friends? In Jesus? Tell him. Not four loved ones can be found? Maybe two? One? No one? You feel so alone. And so we will continue our imagining.

See yourself lying paralyzed on the ground in the house next door to the house where Jesus is teaching. Although he has no time to eat because of the crowd, imagine him tapping Peter on the shoulder, saying: "Get me through this crowd, Peter. I have someone who needs me." Watch Peter bulldoze through the crowd, officiously crying: "Make way, make way!" Jesus blinks in the sunlight. You can see him through your open door. He turns as though looking for someone. He sees you and walks directly through your door. His hand rests on your arm as he crouches down next to you. Can you feel the pressure of his hand on your arm? How does he smell? What do his eyes convey? Now he asks you to talk to him, to tell him how you feel, to cry bitterly, angrily, to weep sorrowfully because you feel so abandoned. Let all your emotions pour out into his ear and into his heart. Watch him listen to you with such respect for your feelings. After he listens, he asks if he may touch you. If you agree, feel his hand as he strokes your arm, kneads your shoulder muscles, brushes your hair off your forehead. His hands are healing, his touch so loving. As he often does, now he asks you what it is that you want. Tell him.

Jesus feels and deals with grief (based on John 11:1-45). Watch Jesus' response to the death of Lazarus. As you watch and listen to him, let your personal grief(s) surface as well. Jesus had been summoned to Bethany because his friend Lazarus was so sick it seemed he would die.

Jesus did not act immediately. He needed some time to work through his feelings with his Father. And so he prayed: "Oh God, I just don't think I can do it. This feels too much like Joseph's death. Strangers I can help, but I get so caught into Martha and Mary. I lose my objectivity—whatever that is. No. What I mean is, Father, I HATE DEATH! I can't bear it. The truth is, I lose my heart. Why should Lazarus die? He's way too young, and too needed by Martha and Mary. Who will provide for them if he's gone? This is a mess, and I want to stay far, far away."

Jesus lowered his arms and then sat back against a tree trunk. This was no mountain for prayer, just a small tree, a bit away from the campsite the disciples had set up. Martha had summoned him yesterday. He smiled in the dark at her imperious ways, and this time, her quite indirect way. She hated to admit she needed him. "Lord, the one whom you love is sick."

Against the tree trunk, Jesus sat, hands open on his lap, head turned up, loving the three from Bethany, and without words, letting his Father see the warmth of his memories. Martha and Mary had lived in their father's house; but now that their father was dead, the responsibility for them lay with their brother. Without Lazarus, how could they survive?

As the warmth turned to worry, Jesus made a gesture. Still sitting, he raised his open hands just slightly. "They are yours, Father. Help them. Help me to trust you." His heart quieted and he tried to listen. There was no booming voice of God. No words at all. Just a gradual peace that seeped through him and a small nudging of his heart. To conclude his prayer, he stood, lifted both his hands, up and open, holding his three friends from Bethany in them and saying: "May you bless them, our God, and keep them. May your face shine upon them and give them peace."

Next day, they all headed toward Bethany. Martha met them on the way. Her grief made her furious. "Where were you? If you'd have been here, Lazarus would still be alive. You work wonders for everyone but your friends? Mark my words, Jesus, if this is how you treat your friends, you'll have very few left!"

"Martha." Jesus spoke softly. "I'm sorry. So sorry about Lazarus. You know he is alive with God."

"Fat lot of good that'll do us!" she retorted.

"Martha, let me see what I can do."

"Hah! He's been in the tomb for four days. You raise people now? That's a new one!"

"God does the raising, Martha. Although it surely seems that God has been using me to bring life wherever I go. I'm here now. Can we go to the tomb?"

"Look. I know you are the Christ, God's anointed one. Come to the house. I'll see you there." She turned abruptly and stomped off down the road in the town. She found Mary there, in tears, as usual.

"The Teacher has finally arrived and he wants you. Maybe you can move his heart. He's so imperious and detached with me. Men!" she sputtered.

Mary got up quickly and hurried out to meet Jesus. Those who had come to mourn with her followed her down the road. Jesus hadn't moved from the spot where Martha had left him. He was still stunned by her rage. He did not have the benefit of mountain or dark for prayer.

He had simply faced away from his companions, looking toward Jerusalem's Mt. Zion. "I lift up my eyes to the mountain. When will help come to me? My help is in you, my Lord, my God. You nudged me, our God, and I let myself be nudged. You want me to face this death head on? It's opening the old wounds of my father's death, my helplessness, my mother's wailing, my grandpa's rage at you. I don't want to be with Martha and Mary. It hurts too much. Oh, help me. The billows of grief sweep over me."

His prayer was interrupted by Mary's hand on his shoulder. He wheeled around, saw her tear-streaked face and lost all semblance of composure. A deep sob broke from him and he reached for her. Mary's anger was more subtle than Martha's. Rather than receive his embrace, she sank, alone, onto the road, head bowed deeply into her lap, hugging her own shoulders, rocking, moaning softly.

He just looked at her blankly. Then he groaned deep within himself and sat on the road beside her...waiting...

Now, in Ignatian contemplation, you are invited to enter this scene. With whom do you identify? Are you an onlooker, one of the disciples or a mourner? What do you see, hear, sense, feel?

Do you grieve like Martha, covering your deep hurt with officiousness, anger and efficiency? Seeing Jesus' tears over the one you love, how do you feel? Tell him.

Do you grieve like Mary, just a puddle of tears, collapsed on the ground? Jesus doesn't admonish you to pull yourself together and get over it. He sits with you and cries. Tell him how you feel.

Do you grieve like Jesus? Pray his prayers in your own voice. Make up your own prayers of grief, confusion, rage. Whatever you feel, lay before God—just as Jesus did and still does, making intercession for us and for all the brokenhearted.

Are you like Lazarus, feeling so dead in depression, numb, bound so tightly in the winding-cloths that you are paralyzed and suffocating in the tomb? Listen to the wailing and sobs as your family, friends and Jesus approach where you lie so helpless. They want you to live. Try to cry, "Help."

Imagination in prayer not only helps us enter the Gospel

scenes more fully, but it also lets us image and share God's great desires for us and for our world. To share in God's imagination, God's hope for what is possible in this world, to join our deep desires for peace and unity with God's, is to pray—and to pray always. Even confined to house, to wheelchair, to bed, there is no chaining the word of God, nor our power of imagination and desire to effect a new world. This passionate hope is a way of deep union with the passion of God's own heart.

Memories in and as Prayer

In drawing on our senses and our feelings as we entered the two Gospel scenes above, we were also using our memories in prayer. We remembered our grief, we remembered what it was that once paralyzed us and who was with us in our helplessness. For the people of Israel, to remember the acts of God in their community, their families and their own lives was to make that act present again. That is why, each Passover, even today, when the Jewish family gathers for the celebration, they believe and they know that once again, as they remember, God is leading them out of slavery and into freedom. It is that Jewish belief which sparks our Christian belief that when the Christian community remembers the dying and rising of Jesus, that the cross and Resurrection are present again in our midst. We proclaim, in the present tense: "Dying you destroy our death, rising you restore our life." Remembering these events of salvation, this mystery of faith, makes it present in our here-and-now community.

We can use a memory of a past hurt, slight, anger, fear, resentment, and in our imagination see Jesus move into the situation that hurt us, frightened us or angered us. His gospel is a living word, and he is still with us to bring Good News wherever pain sticks in our throat, our heart, our lives. He wants to free up whatever is paralyzed and dead in us, as well as to heal the memories that keep the water and the sunshine of his love from penetrating the hard crust of our soil.

For Reflection and Prayer

Just as in the story of the paralytic and Lazarus, image yourself in a Gospel scene, one of your favorites. Maybe it is a healing passage and you put yourself into the sick/lame/blind/deaf person's place. Let Jesus squat close to you on your pallet and listen to the story of whatever still hurts you from the past. How does he look? Smell? Sound? How does he listen, and then how does he respond? After he responds to your hurt, respond to him.

The above exercise, which can be used anytime a painful memory surfaces, is not only a way to know Jesus more deeply, it is also good psychology. Memories are often healed in a therapist's office by reliving a scene of loss, hurt, fear or anger vividly, talking about it, bringing it into the light and letting all the feelings that surround that painful event come crashing out and into the therapist's office and the therapist's heart. Some of us, even in nursing homes, are fortunate enough to have a therapist or spiritual director with whom to speak, or perhaps a friend or spouse who can listen and not be frightened of our strong emotion. All of us have the most thorough of healers, however, with whom to work through the painful memories: Jesus.

Perhaps like the blind man (Mark 8:22-26) whom we mentioned in Chapter Two, Jesus does not heal us well enough the first time we ask. We keep asking. We can invite him to come right into the scene where we were traumatized as a youngster, or betrayed as a young adult, or cast off by our company, or insulted by our spouse. One elder tells the story of her interest as a five-year-old in gender differences, how she asked a neighbor boy of three to pull down his pants so she could compare him with her brother. The boy's mother came storming over to complain. The girl's mother, embarrassed, dragged her five-year-old out from under the table where she was cowering, pulled down her pants and spanked her in front of the neighbor. This woman spoke through the years to her husband of how her negative attitudes towards sexuality puzzled her because later in her growing up her mother had told her "the facts of life" in a most reverent and beautiful way.

81

One day in a time set aside for prayer, she asked Jesus about her nonappreciation of sex. Instead of a verbal response, she had a flashback to that scene of spanking. Not only the neighbor was hammering at her front door, but right behind the distraught mother came Jesus. He took charge of the scene, and told the two mothers to sit over in the corner. Then he found the frightened child, set her on his lap and asked her about the incident. After she had told him, Jesus assured her that what she had done was quite normal and even praised her curiosity. The woman's husband noted the change in their sexual relationship. The woman, so amazed was she that Jesus could enter her memory so forcefully and heal it, found a spiritual director to help her unpack the experience.

Of course, Jesus enjoys sharing our joyful memories too. One of the rationales for our journal keeping is that too often we forget the wonderful acts of God in our personal, family and community history. If we record these events of grace, then when we are tired or forgetful or discouraged, our rereading of the sacred text of our own life can often bring back not only the memory of God's love, but the feeling of it as well.

For Reflection and Prayer

If you pray the rosary, sometimes, instead of focusing on the joyful mysteries in Jesus' and Mary's life, you might sift through your memories to find the joyful mysteries of your own life. As you pray the Hail Mary's for each of your own mysteries, remember that by reflecting on them, you, like Mary, will be growing in wisdom.

Another time you might search for—or they may leap out at you—five sorrowful mysteries in your life, and ponder them as you pray. It is especially helpful at yet another time to ask the Spirit to call to mind when a sorrowful mystery in your life has been tended by God and turned into a joyful, or even a glorious mystery.

For Reflection and Prayer

If you pray the psalms, you might pray Psalm 107, a song of gratitude for God's work in the peoples' salvation history. We, too, have a history of God's saving work. As you pray the psalm slowly, see whether any of God's work for Israel has also been the story of God's work in your life. For example, when had you lost your way and were wandering, and God led you to a home? When were you miserable because of your sins or the sins of others, and God broke your chains? When were you like the sailors in a storm, thrown to the heavens and then plunged to the sea, and God led you straight to the port you wanted? Let Israel's historical psalms guide you in touching back into your own history with God.

CHAPTER SEVEN

Tending

U p to this point, much of this book contemplates God, our gardener, working in the field of our lives. We are the passive soil that God has been gardening: clearing the ground, preparing it, sowing and growing and tending us. Now we respond to God's initiative with tending of our own. Julian of Norwich, medieval English mystic, invites all of us to be "gardeners of the spirit."

The best response to God's initiative is to be what we are, fully human, fully alive, and becoming more so as we age. We are to acknowledge our creaturehood, our dependence on God, and then to use the whole of our self to tend our bodies, minds, wills, imaginations, relationships and even the planet.

Tending the Self

To tend the self first of all is to remember in whom we are grounded, in whom we live and move and have our being (Acts 17:28). Before we can tend ourselves, we reaffirm that God initiates all good growth, that it is the Spirit, not our accomplishment, who keeps our spirits joined with God. Our first step in tending the self, then, is to open to the Spirit and respond with mind, will, body, emotions, imagination and memory.

We let the Spirit wake us up, keeping us sharp mentally and emotionally. Not only spiritual exercises, but mental and physical exercises, exercising our imaginations, memories and wills, can help us stay alert as we age. As Betty Friedan reviewed studies of aging she discovered:

• that the decline in our various capacities as we age are neither

universal nor predictable; we are not biologically
programmed;

- that mental functioning does not decline, but can actually
  improve;

- that disengagement from social activities was not the pattern
  found among healthy survivors in major longitudinal studies
  of "normal human aging";

- that activity of some complexity, using cognitive skills and
  involving choice, is a crucial clue to longevity and vital aging;

- that an accurate, realistic, active identification with one's own
  aging, rather than passive resignation to it or denial of it, is
  also key, even to longevity.

Friedan with this positive attitude wondered whether "age in
fact, may offer the opportunity to develop values and abilities,
for each of us and for society, that are not visible or fully
realized in youth" (*The Fountain of Age*, pages 84-85).

Rea's congregation, the School Sisters of Notre Dame, is
participating in a University of Kentucky study of Alzheimer's
disease by donating their brains for research after they die.
Most of them amused themselves with word and math puzzles,
games of Scrabble, Trivial Pursuit and Password, read widely
both fiction and nonfiction, were encouraged to slow down
regularly through prayer and meditation, and to improve
circulation through physical exercise. This may have
contributed to a lower incidence of Alzheimer's among them
than among the general population. (A definitive diagnosis of
Alzheimer's is only possible after autopsy of the brain.)

Rowe and Kahn observe in *Successful Aging* that
Alzheimer's disease is not an all or nothing experience because
the plaques and tangles associated with it have been found in
the brains of people without any symptoms. And, they
comment about one Notre Dame sister who did have "a high
count" of brain plaques:

Pathology reports from the widely publicized Nun Study
indicated that Sister Mary, who demonstrated superior

cognitive ability until her death at age 101, had a high
count of neocortical diffuse plaques—second highest
among the first 118 deaths in the Nun Study (page 43).

Rowe and Kahn assert that we, through training and practice,
can increase our cognitive abilities, and "Memory losses
among healthy older people are also reversible with training"
(page 136).

Betty Friedan in *The Fountain of Age* once again bears good
news to us: "The presumed loss of brain cells with age does not
take place in normal aging. Vital new brain connections can
continue to develop until the end of life and even reverse
deterioration. The plasticity of the brain makes either decline or
further growth possible but not programmed in age" (page 92).
In fact, Friedan questions critically the brain tests of memory
and cognitive functions which may be geared to youth
(page 96).

Rea found her own mentor in aging when Sister Philemon,
S.S.N.D., began to teach herself Russian when she was in her
eighties. In the troubled times of the 1960's, Phil thought Russia
might one day control the world. She wasn't worried, she was
prepared. Another School Sister whom Rea was about to visit at
their retirement home didn't hear her approach. Rea was able to
contemplate this bedridden teacher of college physics
contemplating a piece of art in a large coffee-table book open on
her lap. Some thirty years later, Rea has the categories to know
that this woman of powerful left-brain learning was intuitively
developing her right-brain capacity.

As part of the process of integration, we who have made
friends in mid-life with our shadow side, who have developed
both our masculine and feminine qualities, now have the leisure
to tend to the logical and verbal (left) side of our brain or to the
creative (right) side. We are becoming whole.

The Body. Our bodies remain essential to who we are. To tend
to the self is to attend to them. May Sarton reflected on her
body after her stroke: "Youth, it occurs to me, has to do with
not being aware of one's body, whereas old age is often a matter
of consciously overcoming some misery or other inside the

body. One is acutely aware of it" (*After the Stroke,* page 35).

Our bodies usually signal the move from a wellness model of aging, so encouraged by Betty Friedan in *The Fountain of Age,* to the diminishment model of aging, which may indeed become part of our experience unless we die suddenly. Since each of us ages at a unique pace, we will first address specific elements of bodily growth from a wellness perspective, and then from the reality of diminishment.

The Sisters of the Holy Cross, Rachel's community, have summarized some of the foci of wellness. Wellness emphasizes strengths rather than limitations, choices that enliven us rather than protect us. Wellness focuses on the whole person (body, mind, spirit), builds on the positive, moves toward integration. Diminishment, a reality at some point in our aging, is usually focused on the body or the brain, and thus is heavily influenced by the medical model.

Some bodily activities that enhance our wellness are exercise, relaxation techniques, deep breathing, recreation, walking. Exercise, fresh air, sleep and diet play an important role in keeping us healthy. For example, although she is ninety-one, Mrs. Kay Dunphy insists on her daily walk. However, there are no sidewalks in her small New England town, and so sometimes the police find her and guide her home. Out she goes the next day. To celebrate her ninetieth birthday, her daughter found party napkins that proclaimed: "If older is better, then you are magnificent!"

Fresh air is important, as is deep breathing, to keep our brain cells operating. Yet rather than miss their daily walk, some tear briskly around the local mall. The point is to exercise. Researchers were surprised to learn that those who engaged in strenuous physical activity, even the usual homemaking or lawncare chores, "were more likely to maintain their high cognitive function" because of the effect of exercise on the brain, promoting new brain cells (*Successful Aging,* page 133).

Just as we are likely to vacuum regularly on, say, Saturday morning, so we can choose special times to help us remember to exercise. For example, we can do isometric exercises, tensing and releasing large muscle groups, when we are stopped at a red light or in line at the checkout counter.

When diminishment happens, we can still exercise—carefully. Eye exercises, leg exercises, gentle stretching, neck and shoulder rolls can be done in a hospital bed or a wheelchair. Isometric exercises, simply the tightening and releasing of a muscle group, can encourage blood flow. We can even imagine the fresh, oxygenated blood rushing to strengthen our muscles and organs.

Wellness calls for more rest than our urban culture usually allows. If we learn to pace ourselves in the earlier years of our aging, to claim a sabbath each week, and a bit of sabbath rest each day, we will be ready for the leisure "forced" on us in retirement or when the nest is emptied. It may be a myth that we need less sleep as we age. Some of us who have lived harried and hurried younger lives may now be so exhausted in our older age that our bodies crave sleep. "At last I can lie down and go to sleep and then awake, for God has hold of me," we read in Psalm 3:5. The best rule of thumb is to note our mood when awake. If we feel rested during the day, we may indeed not need a lot of sleep.

On the other hand, especially in retirement, our nodding off continually throughout the day, only to lie awake at night, can exacerbate loneliness and worry. Doctors can prescribe inexpensive medicines that help not only sleeping but the mild forms of depression and anxious obsessing that keep some of us awake. The best rule of thumb is to speak honestly with a physician. Here is what Scripture says:

> Honor the physician...
> God has established this profession,
>   giving the doctor wisdom...
> God makes the earth fruitful with healing herbs
>   which the prudent will not neglect....
> Through which the physician can heal pain
> And the pharmacist can prepare medicine.
> (Sirach 38:1-2,4,7)

Diet in a wellness model of aging begins with nutrition. Certain foods such as spinach help slow macular degeneration of the eyes, a common problem as we age. Others, like turkey, provide a natural sedative. Some foods like carrots act as antioxidants, cleansing the blood of radical free cells, believed to cause even something as insignificant as wrinkles. The traditional eight glasses of water a day, as well as a lessening of caffeine, prove even more essential as we age. We have read the news of natives of the Ukraine and Georgia who live long lives, attributed to daily yogurt intake. Another mentor in aging to whom this book is dedicated, Rose Irving, never varied from her morning routine of raisin bran and orange juice.

But gradually we do diminish. Food may lose its appeal as we age. Our taste buds, and the sense of smell that assists taste, seem to wear out. Thus it is important to build healthy habits of nutrition at a younger age. Articles on a balanced diet can be found in almost every magazine. "Meals on Wheels" provides an important service to the homebound. We need to recognize our need for dietary help and act on it. One translation of the first beatitude is "Happy are they who know their need for God." Happy, too, are we who know our need for human help, and all the services provided by state, county, community and church. Knowing our need is a kind of obedience to the Spirit. We pray to know the truth, not to deny reality.

When the Spirit reveals how dependent we have become— in reality—we learn to obey the reality of our weakened bodies, our tired minds, our inability to do as much as we once did. Obedience to reality is a sign of wisdom.

The Mind. In the wellness model of aging, because our minds crave learning, filling that mental hunger keeps us intellectually sharp. Some people take advantage of Elderhostel, a program usually held on a college campus in various parts of the country, that combines classes, field trips and a chance to form new relationships. Some find tours, even overseas, geared for seniors, and others participate in community theater and other art events close to home. Cable TV's History Channel, Discovery Channel and programs like *Biography* make audiovisual learning a delight. Less expensive are the Public Broadcasting programs like *National Geographic* and *Nova.* Even *Jeopardy* keeps us mentally alert. Video stores and video sections of the library make vicarious travel possible, with series of travel videos, usually less expensive, and often free from the library. Community centers may sponsor a bridge club, chess competitions, or classes on how to use a personal computer or surf the World Wide Web.

Should we be in a more diminished phase of aging, however, there are ways to keep on exploring and learning. If our eyes are failing, books-on-tape, available from most libraries, can provide the entertainment of a novel or the learning of a language, history or biography. Listening to a professional actor read a nonfiction selection or Shakespeare provides both entertainment and learning. It can be especially integrating to hear or watch the history we have actually lived through.

In *Successful Aging*, Rowe and Kahn suggest that we take our time with new learnings, building patience with ourselves: "...to learn new skills in their old age it is essential that they are allowed to go at their own pace, have time to practice the skills and not be in competition and thus embarrassed by the younger ones' speed" (page 22).

May Sarton offers a remedy for the memory frustrations of even younger elders who are stressed: developing a routine. A certain place we always put our keys on coming home. Filling the pill box designed for a week's doses on Saturday night right after a favorite TV program. Sarton writes:

> Never have I been more aware than in these last months how life-preserving my routine is. The day becomes a series of stepping stones.... So the routine makes a frame and I feel that there is a next stepping stone to force me to do something, helps me get through the hours when I feel simply ill, passively and hopelessly ill. (*After the Stroke*, pages 66-67)

The Will. A wellness model of aging means that we stay in charge of the decisions that pertain to our well-being for as long as we are able. Although it may seem easier at first to surrender to the care of another—an attentive son, a solicitous daughter— the more we exercise our own choices, the stronger our wills become even into old, old age. Many women, especially, have never been socialized to take charge of themselves. More women, however, even sheltered and protected women, learn quickly after becoming widows how to handle the checkbook, call the plumber, get the house re-roofed. And they thrive, whereas more men die more quickly after the death of their spouses. The movie *The Cemetery Club* offers an example of the importance of strengthening our wills as we age: Esther learns to drive once her husband dies, whereas Ben, on the death of his wife, gives up the excitement of police work and settles for driving a cab.

The Imagination. One fifty-year-old woman has just discovered the joy of Ignatian contemplation, imaginatively entering into the Gospel scenes with all our senses open and alert as we see Jesus heal and teach, suffer and be raised. This woman has recently put her mother into a nursing home and is still grieving that decision. She travels three hours each week to visit her for a few days, and three hours home again, but now she has Jesus as her front-seat passenger. She lets Gospel stories unfold in her imagination as she drives, and joins him in his living and loving. Then, she talks over with Jesus all her feelings, desires, problems and joys. And he talks back. She has a doctorate in psychiatric nursing and is well trained to distinguish hallucinations. This experience of Jesus sharing her life, of herself as a companion of Jesus, has energized her during this difficult time. She expects that this imaginative interaction with the living Word of God, Scripture and Jesus, will carry well into old age. "When I can no longer see or hear or maybe even move, I will have him in my imagination, loving me, sharing my thoughts and feelings and desires. What hope that gives me!"

Tending Relationships

All meaning is in relationship, claimed two of the twentieth century's great thinkers, the Jew Martin Buber, and the Christian Gabriel Marcel. "...[F]aith, hope and love. And the greatest of these is love, " claims the Jewish Christian Paul in his First Letter to the Corinthians (13:13).

The meaning and the mission given to each one of us in our baptism is to continue the meaning and mission of Jesus. We were "christened," inserted into Christ so that "no longer I live, but he lives in me" (Galatians 2:20), slowly, gradually, day by day. Jesus spent his thirty or so years on earth proclaiming good news, preaching peace in the voice of God (Acts 10:36), healing hearts through a love that sought out and included the discarded and neglected of society. In his final hours he prayed that all might be one, we in him, him in us, all of us in union with each other. "By this will all people know that you are my disciples, that you love one another" (John 13:35).

Two thousand years later we who are baptized are continuing his mission of loving, making one, being one, praying for unity. Whether in our aging we are healthy or bedridden, with or without education, well thought of or ignored by society, our mission stems from our identification with Jesus from the time of our baptism. As Jesus continued to set captives free even while hanging on the cross ("Father, forgive them"; "today you will be with me in paradise"), so we are to carry on his mission—bringing good news, praying for peace, offering healing love to our neighbors both near and far—until our dying breath. When we ache, are in excruciating pain, have tubes dangling from every orifice, can no longer speak, we are still spiritually empowered to carry on his mission of fostering relationship. We may never see the results on this earth, but recall that Jesus didn't either.

For Reflection and Prayer

Imagine yourself, if you are able, in this drastic scene of suffering and dying just described above. You may not be able to pray as you once did. Just to breathe may be your only offering. Now imagine yourself breathing in (even via a ventilator) the peace of God, the shalom, the Spirit, the dunamis, the power of God. In your relative good health, breathe in deeply. Feel now the peace and power of God's Spirit rushing through your blood stream, consoling you. Then breathe out.

Breathe out a smile. Feel what happens to your face, to the tensions that most of our faces unconsciously hold. How does this smile feel to you physically? Breathe in peace, breathe out a smile. In, out. Now breathe out your smile on one of your loved ones, then another and so on. Breathe out a smile on one person whom it is difficult for you to love. On another who causes you discomfort. Breathe out a smile on a whole group of people who are hard to understand or love or even tolerate. Smile on them with the very smile of the risen Christ smiling in your heart.

A spiritual exercise like the one above, breathing in *shalom* (the peace that is God's will, health, wholeness and integrity) and breathing out a smile, practiced frequently, prepares us for the times when our prayer may seem dry, dull, depressed or just impossible. If we become familiar with its rhythm now, if a time comes when we may not be able to control even our face muscles, our heart will know the rhythm well and will smile interiorly.

Our mission to love does not end with either acute or chronic illness and/or debility. Even if we are fairly isolated as we age, it is our call and our gift "to love as Jesus loves." And even if we are still playing tennis at seventy, we are indeed too weak to "accomplish" that love on our own. Love is not our work. Love is the Spirit poured into our hearts in Baptism. Love has been grown in us by the Spirit all through our lives. The Spirit, however, can only love if we are open to deepening our love of God, our selves and every other creature. Even in relative isolation from flesh and blood beings, we can contemplate and love and smile out peace on our distant neighbors, the ones we see burned out on the local news, the victims of an air strike, the children terrorized by a gunman.

How are we to love as Jesus loved/loves? The word *love* is so wrung of meaning in our society, and the word *charity* so condescending a replacement, that we look to Scripture for freshness and specificity. Perhaps no words of Saint Paul are so revered even in the secular world as his famous hymn (1 Corinthians 13:4-7) about love:

Love is always patient and kind;
Love is never jealous nor boastful nor conceited,
never rude nor selfish.
Love does not take offense and is not resentful.
Love takes no pleasure in other people's sins,
but delights in the truth.
Love is always ready to forgive, to trust, to hope
and to endure whatever comes.

This description of the specifics of loving well may be difficult in our youth when our patience is short, when our ambitions push us rudely to become "number one," when we secretly rejoice that the hypocrisy of another, especially a rival, is exposed, when trusting others seems naive. If we do not tend patience and kindness in midlife, we may discover as we age, patience growing thin. Kindness may be in such short order toward us that we may hoard it, and hide away for ourselves what kindness we can give. We may be jealous of the success, wealth and especially health of others in our age group. We may recite to ourselves our resentments and the sins of others almost daily. We may be amazed at how rude we can be, and feel somewhat out of control as our "nice" facade is eroded by chronic pain. There is no need to judge ourselves harshly. Indeed, we are humbled to remember that this love we are called to, missioned for, is not our accomplishment.

It is precisely as we know how weak and self-centered our loving is that we know how desperately we need a savior, someone to set us free from the shackles of our subtle selfishness. Jesus offers us a model of how to pray in just such a situation: "Lord, be merciful to me, a sinner" (Luke 18:13). And this person, mumbling in the back pew, went home justified.

Jesus, who stands before the face of God, prays for us continually. The Spirit, love poured into our hearts, puts our unutterable groanings into words that God understands (Romans 8:26). Jesus and his Spirit love through us, through our nagging arthritis pain, our fear of dying, our inability to climb stairs, our helplessness. Theirs is the power that makes us so powerful in our weakness.

For Reflection and Prayer

When might Mary, as she aged through her fifties, sixties, seventies, eighties, have been tempted to impatience and unkindness? To jealousy and boasting? To a curt remark or an act of selfishness? Remember, to feel the feeling is not to sin, but to be tempted. Both she and Jesus were tempted in every way like us (Hebrews 4:15). When memories of the torture and rejection her son endured recurred, how did she deal with feelings of hatred and resentment, so many years later? Don't think about how she handled these temptations; ask her directly, and then be silent and listen for some response to bubble up from deep within you. This "bubbling up" is one way the Spirit, living deep in your unconscious, can teach you.

In the last letter the aging Saint Paul wrote, he crafted another hymn to love. Here he marshals participles, action words, to describe our mission to love:

> Let love be genuine, authentic,
> Shrinking from evil, clinging to good,
> Loving warmly, affectionately,
> Preferring one another,
> Not slothful but zealous, burning in spirit,
> Serving the Lord,
> Rejoicing in hope,
> Enduring in affliction,
> Continuing steadfastly in prayer,
> Sharing the needs of the saints,
> Practicing hospitality. (Romans 12:9-13)

Love for Paul was neither an ethical code nor a moral system. Love was God's gift to and in him. Paul had to learn not to measure his progress in good works, but to trust that God was deepening his love moment by moment. We could view this hymn to love as a checklist for how we are doing, for taking our spiritual pulse. To what advantage? To boast? To thank God "that I am not like other people for I fast twice a week, I tithe, I do not commit adultery as these others do" just as the Pharisee in Jesus' parable "thanked" God (Luke 18:12)? To wallow in our "no-goodness" or our "not-good-enoughness"? It is futile to try to know even if we are living in the state of grace. If we delude ourselves, thinking we know because we have accomplished love or because we have earned grace, then we have no need to trust in God's gift of grace. There is a saying that is probably quite true: "Young people think they are holy and they are not; middle-aged people think they are not holy and they are not; old people think they are not holy and they are." Holiness, spiritual growth, deepening of love is not ours to work at and measure. It is all God's gift (Ephesians 2:8).

For Reflection and Prayer

Speak with Mary about how much you want your loving to be real, genuine. Ask her how she became ever more authentic, and that means ever more who she is, human, a woman—not angelic and not divine. How did Mary become more and more affectionate as she aged? Don't think about it but ask her directly and listen. As her body was breaking down, how did she keep her spirit on fire for God and the good news? Ask her to teach you some specific ways an older person can serve the Lord, share the needs of the community and practice hospitality. For example, Mary did not have a telephone, but is it not hospitable to phone the shut-ins in your community? Ask Mary and the Spirit who always fills her—and you—to teach you how to love.

Close Relationships

Some fifty- or even seventy-year-olds are still caring for their parents. This can be a burden, but it has also been a joy for those who have learned to demythologize their parents and relate with them as real people. Sometimes we have canonized one parent and demonized the other. Sometimes we have never worked through their role of authority in our early lives. We may never have become our own person, but are still trying to live up to what our parents expected of us. The good news? If our parent(s) are still mentally alert, it is never too late to change that relationship.

In Rea's story of Mr. Ago's death and the creation of a new family through it, part of that family was Jane's mother, Josie. When Josie was about eighty years old, she made a journey we all thought would rip her apart, closing her home in the Boston area to move to Maryland, nearer Jane. Josie was happy to come closer. But that would mean a change in their relationship. Jane decided that she would always speak the truth to her mother— carefully, gently, but the truth. No more taking care of her mother's feelings, for that was a way of patronizing her. No more hiding away Jane's various activities lest her mother disapprove. Josie was, as many an Irish mother is, quite able to manipulate her children to get her way. Jane changed the rules. Direct communication would be the new rule in their relationship. At first there were squalls on the horizon. Gradually Josie realized that Jane was offering her respect, the respect of one adult with another. Gradually they became two women friends. Josie changed a decades-old pattern of relating with her daughter, and did so with delight.

Those who lose their parents when they are young feel the excruciating separation, but are spared the pain of watching them decline. Those who lose their parents in their own old age may be better prepared, but many have forged deeper bonds. "I have had my mother all my seventy-three years," an older woman responded when some well-wisher told her in her grief, "It was to be expected, you know."

One of our respondents wrote a poignant letter to her siblings after their mother's death. We quote portions of it here:

> I wonder how Mom made the leap from "I'm so glad to be on this earth," just hours after her surgery to "I want to go to another place; I want to go to heaven," just twenty-four hours later. I wonder if Mom knew how much she meant to each one of us, how very essential she was (is) to our existence, individually and as a family...
>
> I know that ultimately Mom chose to let go...that she wasn't afraid to die. The first thing she said after all treatment was discontinued was, "Tell all my kids that I love them and I know that they love me." So if you think you didn't say it to Mom enough times, she knew it. She knew it from every story she ever told about each of us, from every moment she savored, from her absolute pride in each of us no matter how lousy we sometimes felt about ourselves....

I remember that Mom had a great devotion to Saint Anne, whom legend names as grandmother of Jesus. Mom was shocked to learn that there was nothing about Saint Anne in the Bible because she thought the grandmother role too important to go unmentioned....

She told the doctor that she didn't want any more treatment. When he came in to pronounce her dead, he said, "Your mother made a very courageous decision today." We may have to let go of Mom in some very real and painful ways, but I believe she will never let go of us.

Besides our parents, no one has known us as long as our siblings. While we may not have lived with them or even near them for forty or eighty years, we may have tended those relationships and now can reap a rich harvest of love—and pain. Often, we do expect the death of our parents, the older generation. When one of our own age group in the family, especially a younger sibling, dies, however, the shock can cut through any denial of death in us. Or as older siblings die, one after the other, until we are alone, the most elderly now in our family, what a loneliness! Who has been there, where we have been in such formative years, the old family home, the schoolyard, the streetcar line, the grocery store where Mama shopped, the station where Dad used to hop off the train? Who now can remember Grandma's crinkled eyes and the smell of Uncle Joe's pipe? Who "does" Christmas as our family did so long ago? And whatever happened to Grampa's hand-carved nativity set? Our siblings are gone. We are very alone.

For Reflection and Prayer

In your journal, list each one of your siblings, living or dead. Then speak each one's name out loud, very slowly. Breathe in peace, and as you breathe out a smile, picture that brother or sister. Picture her/him at different stages of life. Smile God's shalom. Or if your sibling has already died, image him or her smiling on you, breathing on you God's shalom. Some siblings evoke a smile from us. Memories of others create pain. A broken relationship, a fight, a silent estrangement, a real wickedness like incest, a lording it over, a withholding of support and love, an ancient jealousy. What would the Spirit lead us to do with these relationships? Ask the Spirit. No "shoulds" allowed, for the Spirit, who teaches us, creates fresh ideas. If that split-off sibling has already died, he or she is with God. Our brother or sister can now know us truly, can understand the pain of our separation or the depth of our wound. They love us with God's own unconditional and steady faithfulness now. They want, they need reconciliation with us. They are alive with God. Picture them, speak with them, pour out your heart, and then listen to them. Practice this form of prayer periodically until you can sense that, indeed, the Spirit has mended the bonds between you.

We warned you not to let a "should" rule your relationship with a cut-off sibling. There is wisdom in the Twelve-Step program's caution to make amends only if the time is ripe. The Spirit will guide you, because what could be closer to the heart of Jesus than that all brothers and sisters be reconciled?

Many of us have left our family of origin to create our own new family, and again, those relationships may be tensed with years and even decades of pain. If we have been praying for the Spirit to teach us truth, not to let us deny our sin, gradually we will be healed of needing to have the relationship our way, healed of the wounds we have inflicted as well as what we have suffered from our spouses or children. If there is estrangement yet in our family, we can daily "send" Jesus, the light, to "melt the frozen, warm the chill," as the sequence for Pentecost prays. Again the twelve-step program cautions us that sometimes distance is necessary where a particular relationship is unhealthy. Yet we can always pray.

When the risen Jesus returned to his friends, he showed them his wounds. How wonderful at this time in our life when our own unhealed wounds may haunt our memories and even keep us from sleep, that Jesus would come to us, his friends, with wounds in his hands and his heart. They no longer throb with pain, but stream glory and grace and healing, and they are stretched out to us and those whom we love.

For Reflection and Prayer

Image this risen Christ holding out his hands to you. Pay attention (yet another name for contemplation) to his wounds. When you are convinced that there is healing in his hands, bring before him each wound in your life that still needs to be lightened. See him tip his hands over each person, each situation that needs healing. See the glory and grace and light pour over the person, drench the situation. Breathe deeply, and sigh. There is hope for healing in this shining of the sun! You may choose to bring only one event or relationship to him today, another tomorrow. Go at your own pace. He is in no hurry, and will wait until you are ready.

Some of our deepest and still tender wounds come from failed marriages. One woman described the pain of her divorce as being like shrapnel speeding throughout her whole body as her heart exploded. The marriage relationship is so complex. Sometimes years later families are still broken apart by recriminations and siding with one parent or the other. It may help to know that alcoholism is a disease, that depression is a disease, that perhaps even incest is a disease and not just a failure of willpower. "If only he really loved us, he would _____." Fill in the blank: stop drinking, get out of bed in the morning, leave our daughter alone. Disease is not a failure to love. Nor does our love cure. As therapist Martha Manning writes in *Undercurrents*, her personal story of depression, if the love of her family could have cured her, she need never have been sick. But love, even the most mature and faithful love, is not enough to heal a variety of hormonal and chemical imbalances in the human brain.

In tending relationships begun long ago, we need to attend, too, to our current relationships: a spouse who no longer recognizes us because of her brain tangles; a spouse so much more mellow and open in older age; a spouse still hungry for the warmth of intertwined bodies; a spouse still needing appreciation for the special dinner or the fixed faucet. "For twenty-five years I've darned your socks," the wife in *Fiddler on the Roof* sings, "Do I love you?!" So tell him, already! Everyone needs to hear those three little words, even our life partner, perhaps even our God!

In October of 1968, long before anyone used the term "Alzheimer's" disease, Rachel's foster mother, Rose O'Donnell, wrote to her about caring for her husband, Bart. In the last week before this book's deadline, Rachel came across this letter. We include it, partly because we always wonder why Rachel found it just now, partly because Rose's small details paint such a graphic picture of pain for the couple, and mostly because so much of Rose's suffering is what so many of us, whether as spouses or children, can identify with. We include it too, because so many of us fear for our own sanity as we age. Saint Ignatius Loyola's prayer: "Take, Lord, my understanding..." may be the hardest prayer for us to pray.

Sister Rachel, my very own darling:

Do please forgive me for not writing sooner. Somehow I'm finding it so hard to write letters. In the first place, I don't have much to write about, and when I do sit down to write Bart is with me, and I'm up and down lighting his Camels.

Bart's health is pretty good. By that, he eats three meals a day and will sleep well if I'm in the next bed. So I go to bed early. He turns in between five and six, and will be up and down until I turn in between eight and nine o'clock. If I don't go I find I get cross, and that will get me nowhere. He will just cry. I'm sure he finds the days very long and not much fun. Now when he tries to tell me something the words will not come out, and like a child he will get upset.

His dreams are wild and so upsetting. He cries out three or four times a night. In the daytime, if I leave him just for a few seconds, he will have one of the spells like when you were here. I shop once a week and then my nephew will take me. I'm back in three-quarters of an hour. The hard part is he will ask me: "Are you Mom or Rose?"

The doctor said I'm very lucky he can get up and down stairs and to the john. I left him one day to get something from the backyard, and he let his cig fall in the chair. You should have seen the smoke, and he still is in

102

the chair, tears running down his face. He still didn't know what happened. It took ten years off my life. Well, maybe just two years.

Well, all in all, I'm very thankful he has no pains. He doesn't see very well and I'm sure his hearing is going. Well, enough about us. Oh, yes, I'm fine. My family are all well. I don't see as much of them as I hate to have them see Bart and he not know them. Then I'm not much fun for company. I'll try to make my letter more cheerful.

All our love,
Mom and Bart

Those elders who live in the light have tended not only their old friends, but have reached out to make new friends. A change of neighborhood, or even city, offers new neighbors, new church friends. A new friendship might grow from a grief support group, or a parish leisure club. When Josie Ago moved to Maryland at eighty, she continued to live alone. However, her ninetieth birthday party was jammed with her new neighbors and friends, and her funeral almost three years later, with still newer friends.

Josie learned to ask for help. When she lived miles from church in her small Massachusetts town, if she were "feeling poorly," she could not bring herself to ask for a ride on Sunday morning, even though the parish provided a pick-up service for its seniors. Josie changed in Maryland, perhaps because she and her daughter Jane were renegotiating her Yankee independence in many areas of her life. Josie stayed in touch with her former friends, too, using her small resources to phone a special friend up north, and keeping up with cards. She spent her time visiting and fostering relationships rather than watching daytime TV.

As we age, our true feelings about children surface. Perhaps we no longer have the energy to keep up a facade. One set of siblings realized that although their father protested his love for them as children, how much he wanted children, it was just a family script. When he married again after a brief grief for his first wife, his own children and grandchildren were somewhat neglected. Others of us rejoice that we can play with grandchildren without having to be responsible for their total care and training. We can contemplate them more easily for just who each one uniquely is. Still others, sadly, have their grandchildren thrust upon them constantly, from babysitting that cuts into the grandparent's continuing personal development, to that total care needed when the children's parent is drugged or drunk or in prison. If we do not freely volunteer to watch our grandchildren, it is normal to feel resentment. We can find grace by working through the resentment.

For Reflection and Prayer

Let us imagine that Mary of Nazareth finds herself in just such a situation. Two of her grandchildren are left with her for total care shortly after Pentecost. How does she pray out of that situation? She is no Pollyanna, remember. How then does, can her risen Son, still alive and praying with her, for her, support her? How can, does she reconfigure her gifts for mission and ministry so as to include these two young people? Ask Mary how to deal with this impingement on your freedom, your retirement, your leisure.

Many seniors find that volunteering can be a kind of thank-offering for their good health and abilities. One of our friends, once he retired, volunteered for a particular piece of the St. Vincent DePaul Society's work in his parish. Because he no longer had to rise early, and could always catch a nap later, he volunteered as the contact person with the city's bus station. Now, when a person or family arrives in town, lost or hungry or without a bed, Bob can be counted on at any hour to pick them up and find them food and shelter. His wife is his support in these ventures.

Some couples are most supportive of their spouse's volunteer activities, their building new relationships and fostering new ones. In fact, it is healthy for those in a long-term marriage to have differing hobbies, volunteer activities and even sets of friends. If there is no differentiation in the marriage one may be jealous of the other's new activities and relationships. One may even sabotage the very interest that keeps one partner alert, alive and young at heart. Marriage counseling is always a possibility as we age. After all, we don't have many role models for how to be married for fifty, sixty or seventy years.

The last relationship to tend may be one that has eased the grief of many a widow or widower who has lost a human companion of forty or sixty years. The children may be scattered across the country and even the world, but the dog, the cat still call from us our generativity. Such creatures are totally dependent on our good grace and offer unconditional loving in return. Dogs are such warm companions, and even literally pull us out of our bed or our chair to tend to their needs. Walking a dog provides daily exercise, which keeps our brains functioning better, our lungs and hearts pumping.

Isolation is a large risk factor as we age. While human contact is preferable, Rowe and Kahn emphasize that nonhuman relating is important too. They give the example of an eighty-two-year-old whose garden and dog provide life-giving activity and relationship. These interactions counteract anomie, the loneliness that can eventually kill (*Successful Aging*, pages 155-156).

Tending Our Earth

There is a new theology today that Francis of Assisi, and even those who preceded him, intuited. Every creature, living or inorganic, is a sign of God, a bearer of God's life. God can be found in all things.

> In the quiet curve of evening, in the sinking of the days,
>   in the silky void of darkness, you are there.
> In the lapses of my breathing, in the space between
>   my ways,
>   in the crater carved by sadness, you are there.
>
> In the rests between the phrases, in the cracks between
>   the stars,
>   in the gaps between the meaning, you are there.

In the melting down of endings, in the cooling of the sun,
in the solstice of the winter, you are there.

In the mystery of my hungers, in the silence of my rooms,
in the cloud of my unknowing, you are there.
In the empty cave of grieving, in the desert of my dreams,
in the tunnel of my sorrow, you are there.

"You Are There" by Julie Howard
Copyright Order of St. Benedict, Liturgical Press, Collegeville

This is not the pantheism we may have been warned against.
God is not the dog or the tree or the soil. Theologically we have
coined a new term: panentheism. Panentheism means that God
is in the dog, the tree, the soil. This realization calls us to
reverence every speck of creation. Once we were taught that
human beings were the crown of creation and that we were to
dominate the earth and its "lesser" creatures. This new theology
instructs us that we share the earth as a community of
creatures, not lording it over any one or any thing.

Tending Our Earth

We live in a moment when it is hard to ignore the reality of the
oneness of our world and the impact we have on our
environment by the way we live. In 1975 the English scientist
James Lovelock offered a new hypothesis about earth and its
interrelatedness. Called the Gaia theory after the Greek earth
goddess, he hypothesizes that instead of being an inanimate
hunk hurtling through space, our Earth is in fact an elaborate
living organism whose tending and balance is required in order
to sustain the abundance of life in all its many forms and
species. The stunning pictures of our Earth taken by astronauts
from outer space which reveal a beautiful blue and white
sphere suggests this unity and harmony. There are no signs of
national or tribal boundaries, simply an undivided wholeness.
As the children's song reflects, "It's a small world after all."
And it is a world that since the beginning of the Industrial
Revolution has been raped and pillaged with varying degrees
of consciousness in the name of business and material growth.

The time has come for us to tend our Mother Earth.

Theologian Sally McFague images our planet as the very body of God. And as Schachter-Shalomi reminds us: "As both older and younger people learn to find fulfillment in non-material ways and consume less of the Earth's resources, they reduce the damage inflicted on the environment and become willing collaborators in healing the planet" (*Age-ing to Sage-ing*, page 21).

Environmentalists make us more and more aware of the ramifications of ignoring the needs of the earth. We can no longer plead ignorance and abandon our responsibility to live on this earth in a reverent way. We must become better stewards of this most basic treasure or else the earth handed on to future generations will be ravaged beyond imagination.

We are making our Mother Earth ill with the wanton destruction of the rain forests. This deforestation contributes to global warming. We dump billions of tons of toxic waste into landfills; from there it finds its way to water supplies both on the earth and beneath its surface into its aquifers. By our greedy consumption of fossil fuel we have polluted our air and depleted this resource. Overdevelopment of land without regard to the needs of environmental balance threatens erosion, which has long-range implications for the increasing global need for food.

We remind ourselves again that theologian Sally McFague images our planet as the very body of God. Scientist/philosopher/mystic Pierre Teilhard de Chardin, S.J., proclaims this good news and possibility for us as we, too, contemplate our Earth: "Throughout my life, through my life, the world has little by little caught fire in my sight until, aflame all around me, it has become almost completely luminous from within...Such has been my experience in contact with the earth..." (*The Divine Milieu*, page 14).

What can we do to share this vision? We can treat every created thing with reverence. In our personal lives we can learn to live more simply, consuming less, practicing recycling. We can become involved in local or national groups working to heal the Earth. We can write letters urging responsible laws and policies in our government. And of course we can pray for the healing of our Mother Earth and to the living Spirit of God who resides in every form of life, in every created thing.

CHAPTER EIGHT

Bearing Fruit

The Greek root of the word *generativity* simply means bearing, but in spiritual and psychological life, it means that we bear fruit. As Psalm 92 proclaims, we are "heavy with fruit, even in old age." Bearing fruit is what Jesus passionately desires for all his friends, including us, on the night before he died: "...Every fruitful branch God prunes, that it might be more fruitful yet.... You cannot bear fruit unless you remain united with me.... This is my Father's glory: that you may bear fruit in plenty, and so be my disciples" (John 15:1, 4, 8).

It is for bearing fruit that we are called and chosen (John 15:16). Bearing fruit is the biblical word. Generativity is the developmental task, according to psychologist Erik Erikson, of mid- to late-adulthood, both learning how and then passing along to future generations what we have gathered in life: lessons, resources, experiences. It is the ability to nurture and support others, an ability to continue to give birth to new ideas from one's own inner wellspring, and to spark new ideas in others. It is the gift of wisdom handed on for the building up of Christ's body and the whole human race. It leads, in both human and spiritual development, to becoming all that God hopes for us. Erikson will name that "integration"; Jeremiah, the prophet, will name it *shalom*, meaning integrity and God's will.

For those who are parents, generativity is part of parenting well. It is more than this, however, both for parents and for those who have never parented. There are many and varied ways of being generative at all ages. Generativity at midlife often presents a lifelong opportunity for growth and Christian service. For example, Jonathan Daneski was featured in the

Capital Dance Connection. At seventy-five, this Trinitarian Brother is characterized by the grinning photo and the headline: "Meeting the Needs of the Moment." For thirty-seven years Jonathan has visited the elderly, the poor and abandoned to discover and meet their needs:

> ...from grocery shopping to making repairs around the house or just providing companionship. He is a hospice volunteer.... With his limited time (and money) he is resourceful about finding time and places to dance.... [Jonathan says:] "Dancing is the best way to slow the aging process because the whole person is involved in celebrating life.... I want to live life to the fullest. Celebrate life as much as I am able to."

Renewing Relationships

As we age, one of our great joys is to become almost daily our true self, renewing our relationship with our own reality. There is no need to manage impressions of ourselves, no need for photo opportunities so that the world, and maybe even our friends and family, see our best face. We have worked through the fear of abandonment, which haunted Jesus, too ("Will you also go away?" he asked his disciples in John 6:67). Eugene Bianchi comments, "As an elder you have become in your very body-person a healer of the devastating fear of abandonment because you have transcended its terror to experience a new mode of belonging to all" (*On Growing Older*, page 25).

Generativity includes a gradual growth toward "belonging to all." As children we negotiated the first three developmental tasks of growing in basic trust, in autonomy and in creativity. Now as we come to what Erik Erikson named the final task, integration, we circle around to a newer, deeper trust, autonomy and creativity. Erikson proposed eight stages of human development, but experience demonstrates that instead of neat progression up stairs and through stages, we often are spiraling down to new depths.

When her mother died, a sixty-five-year-old woman cried, "I feel like I cannot trust the world, life, God. I have lost my autonomy, can't concentrate, can't make a decision. I feel like an infant again." In therapy, as she works through this loss, this grief, the woman will discover that she is not a child, but that her trust, autonomy, creativity, her ability to work, to be intimate, to rediscover her identity has led her to new depths within herself. Her psychological work is a sharing in the transforming work of God. Her life with her mother who has died is still bearing fruit. This work of God, this bearing, goes forward, slowly and painfully, but indeed the "roots are all the deeper and the flowering all the lovelier," in the words of the foundress of the School Sisters of Notre Dame, Blessed Mother Theresa of Jesus Gerhardinger. As this grieving woman regains her trust in life, those things that have fallen apart will be not fixed, but recreated in the process.

Some of the bearing fruit for women, according to Betty Friedan, is discovered in new relationships. Not that men do not value relationships, but Friedan has noticed that older women are free to explore new forms of intimacy—with men, including their own husbands, with other women of any age, with their grandchildren. They can cross traditional lines of age and gender. While some men are glad for hobbies that tap into their creativity in retirement, Friedan found that women "...had continued to develop new purposes and projects long past the conventional age of retirement for men" (page 164).

While exercise and nutrition are important, even essential, those who are preoccupied with their bodies and its functions, pains and diminishments seem to experience the process of aging as a loss. Those who are engaged in relationships, however, no matter how aching their bodies, discover that for them physical discomfort is minimized. Losses pose no threat to the self, and the aging process leads to new ways to be generative, to be in relationship with self, others, the world and God.

In fact, those elderly who were subjects for the MacArthur Foundation research enumerated what kinds of social support they need and which they can offer. First is confiding, the root word of which is *fide*, trust. Then, reassuring, sharing the wisdom they have learned from having gone through many of the same situations. Third, providing care when someone is sick. Finally, they need respect and affection and they need to talk about health issues and other problems (*Successful Aging*, page 162).

Some, eager for optimism, spin the statistics and claim that as the body decays the spirit grows. However, Dr. Lyon in his book, *Toward a Practical Theology of Aging*, counteracts such a dualism, a dividing body and spirit, that has dominated our Western thinking. This pastor reminds us that in Scripture there is no split, no dualism of body and soul. We need not set one part of us over against another, especially in this time for integration.

Reclaiming Creative Power

Bearing fruit means claiming again our creativity, undergirded by new trust and new autonomy. In older age we can be more accepting of the solitude that creativity demands. We can also accept the loneliness that "... is not necessarily rejection or abandonment....[but] an experience that allows us to deepen and to expand our humanity" (Bianchi, page 17). Bianchi means real loneliness, a suffering that has produced creative works of art and relationship. He does not mean, however, what today is so familiar: isolation and alienation. Rather, "Loneliness is a yearning for contact with the deepest realms of ourselves" (page 18). In those depths we reclaim our creative power and energy.

For example, a ninety-six-year-old Irishman, John Harrington of Butte, Montana, button accordion player, has been making music for nine decades. In a city of Italian copper miners, he played the tunes of Ireland to keep his roots fresh (National Public Radio's *All Things Considered*, March 17, 1999). Learning songs from his parents, he also gathered them from County Cork where he returned when he was orphaned. "Everyone was singin' 'em, you know," so he learned over three hundred songs. Back from Ireland, he dug the subways of New York during the day and learned new songs at night. Preserving his heritage in Butte, playing and singing at family and other

Irish gatherings, in 1999 he brought out his first compact disc, *The Celtic Century*.

Harrington's collection of folk songs were themselves collected by the Library of Congress. In Butte John serves as musical archivist and is revered by the younger Irish musicians there. One of Harrington's songs celebrates one of the Irish heroes of the 1916 rising who died on hunger strike, and John comments: "I was over there when he died." A younger Irish musician in Butte notes, "I am learning history, but John is the history." Although he keeps twenty-four bulging scrapbooks, the songs within his head are his dearest treasure. "That old time music is what is keeping me alive."

As we move through the tasks of generativity to integration and back to generativity, we keep discovering new depths of creativity. "To be creative means enhancing our personal integration by pulling together in novel ways the disparate and conflicting strands of our existences" (Bianchi, page 109). In the freedom of our older age, we can play and experiment, explore and create without fear of judgment, our own or others. Because we have come through, have endured, we know now that we are who we are. We share in God's self-designation: "I am who I am" (Exodus 3:14). This claiming of our identity offers us an ever deepening interior creativity and freedom.

Reclaiming Passion

"It is not how old we are, but how we are old," as the saying goes. We can move into old age with resignation and lassitude. We can move into old age with passion, a passion for learning such as John Cardinal Newman evidenced, learning a new language every five years; a passion for noticing, as the elder Claude Monet did, painting the same haystack at different times of day to catch the differences the sun made on the straw's color; a passion for contemplation.

Sister Hester Valentine, S.S.N.D., in her book *Aging in the Lord*, suggests that we spend half an hour looking out our window and listing all the colors we can see. Later, we might ask a friend to join us at the window and be surprised at an even deeper noticing when the two of us compare lists. Or, better yet, she invites us to plant something that we can, with deliberate patience, watch grow (pages 74-75). In his *Sunset and Twilight*, Bernard Berenson assures us that awareness increases as action slows: "While everything else physical and mental seems to diminish, the appreciation of beauty is on the increase" (quoted in Fowler and McCutcheon, page 93).

We might find, as poet Maggy Lindgren does, how simple is contemplation:

> Grace
> Seeing the slender blossom,
> Wild like her love,
> She thought only to stop
> And abide in the earth's whisper
> Until evening consumed the day.

Passion and contemplation coexist very well. As Florida Scott-Maxwell commented: "Age puzzles me. I thought it was a quiet time. My seventies were interesting, and fairly serene, but my eighties are more passionate. I grow more intense as I age" (quoted in Fowler and McCutcheon, page 22).

Claiming New Mission and Ministry

With priorities rearranged, with more leisure, less responsibility for our families and/or work, as elders we may discover new possibilities for mission, an outreach in Christ's name to the world. New possibilities for ministry may open because we have time to notice needs around us. New discoveries of the Spirit's gifts, regular or emergency calls for help from our pastors, all activate a new and deeper ministry, our baptismal vocation for building up the Church community.

We can claim ourselves as the elders in the community. In the early Church community the elderly were sometimes recognized as prophets. Luke's Gospel singles out the eighty-four-year-old prophetess Anna because she was so deeply united with the mind and heart of God through her years of prayer, that she could recognize the power and the promise in the infant she held (Luke 2:36-38). Elders have decades of union with God which give them a seasoned courage to speak the truth with love. They comfort in the name of God those who suffer, who are marked for martyrdom; they encourage and give heart to, strengthening the younger generation's faithfulness. And as elders they challenge, as prophets do, unjust structures in society and even in the Christian community. Their years of union with the mind and heart of God give them the discernment to know when to console and when to critique.

Luke offers three other stories of widows. Although the word for widow in Hebrew means "unable to speak" we hear of the widow who badgered the unjust judge until he gave her what was due her (Luke 18:1-8). It might seem that the widow who "put into the treasury all that she had" was voiceless, but Jesus gave her a mighty voice of generosity to teach us all to give our all (Luke 21:1-4; cf. Mark 12: 41-44). The pain of the silent widow of Nain who walked behind the bier of her dead only son (Luke 7:11-17) was a voiceless cry to Jesus' healing power. She received not only the deep healing of her son's life, but the healing of her social situation. In that culture with no husband and no son to care for her, the woman would have been as good as outcast, a burden on her community. Jesus did not ask her what she wanted or question her faith, as he often did when he healed people. He simply stepped into action, as Jews were meant to do for the sake of widows and orphans.

For Reflection and Prayer

If you are a widow or widower, or have ever lost a spouse to death, if you feel voiceless or left empty now, then try to sit with God and feel together the pain of loss. God, too, is like a widowed one. God understands this loss. Tell God your feelings, and listen to some of God's experience of loss and grief.

To be widowed in the early Christian community was a call to mission and ministry. In the earliest years, the elders were the circle of leaders in the Church. The men sat in council, the women served as the order of widows. For example, when Paul's ship passed near Ephesus for what he sensed would be the last time, he invited not a bishop but summoned the group of Ephesian elders to the seaport for their tearful and affectionate parting (Acts 20: 16,18).

About the time that the presbyters (the Greek term for elders) were becoming the community's priests, about A.D. 180, the order of widows began to die out. The first letter to Timothy is the first to describe their office:

> The status of widow is to be granted only to widows who are such in the full sense....one who is alone in the world, who has all her hope set on God, and regularly attends the meetings for prayer and worship night and day...A widow should not be put on the roll under sixty years of age. She must have been faithful in marriage to one man, and must produce evidence of good deeds performed, showing whether she has care of children, or given hospitality, or washed the feet of God's people, or supported those in distress—in short, whether she has taken every opportunity of doing good. (1 Timothy 5:3, 5-10)

Dr. Bonnie Thurston, who has written a definitive book on widows in the early Church, notes that there is evidence that some widows not only organized the charitable works of the community and made pastoral visits, but the wealthy among them with large homes also conducted the assemblies (page 47). Men and women elders in the early Church would have functioned as the blessing ones, the mediating ones. The priesthood of the faithful flows from our baptismal union with our faithful and compassionate High Priest, Jesus (Hebrews 2:17). He is the only mediator.

The Christian community had suffered from the Jewish priests, the Sadducee party. Thus only Jesus carried the title "priest." Yet early on in the new community, it was clear that the wisdom and fruitfulness of the elders made them mediators in the community. Their long experience of union with the High Priest must have carved out a deep compassion in their hearts, must have kept them faithful in critical political times within the Roman empire. If Christians were known in the first centuries by the love they had one for the other, it may well have been due in part to the mediation of elders which could settle conflict in the community honestly and mercifully.

The one and only priest, Jesus, blessed his community. To bless in Jewish spirituality is to give over all that one is to the one blessed. The risen Christ gives over all that he is to his body, the Church. Especially through the elders the risen Christ continued to bless his young community, for they themselves were a blessing to the newer members. In the centuries when there was no infant baptism, the elders of the community would initiate the young adults into the mysteries of faith, into the mystery of Christ. Christ poured, and continues to pour, all that he is upon these catechumens through the Church's elders, female and male.

The same gifts given to elders in the early Church are available to us in today's community of the faithful. "Ask your elders to enlighten you," we are reminded (Deuteronomy 32:7), where Jewish elders were entrusted with handing onto the next generation the good news of God's saving a people, "finding them in the wilderness, in the wild and howling wasteland, enfolding them with care under God's own wings" (Deuteronomy 32:10-11). We, too, may well have lived through a life that at least at times seemed like a wild and howling wasteland. Indeed, Dr. Bonnie Thurston was led to her study of widows by this modern-day discovery:

> In 1983 a number of magazines ran feature articles on the world's fastest growing poverty group: women. In the United States the poorest group of all was elderly women who had been homemakers and who, as widows, had no pensions or health coverage...[yet in churches]...it was often this very group of older women who were carrying the primary burden of service to and support of their congregations. (*The Widows*, page 7)

Some women serve and support our churches through altar guilds responsible not only for the physical care of the church building but for the needy in the church community, through choir and councils and counting collections. Older men are just as active in their volunteer efforts for the care of the church plant and grounds, sports programs for youth, pancake breakfasts. Many small services, like ushering and altar serving, are now open to both men and women. Many small services, as unnoticed as the widow's mite, call for a grand generosity.

One of the richest ways to bear fruit as an elder in the community may be through our mentoring the newcomers into the congregation. It takes the whole of us, and a deep sharing of our faith's resources, to welcome newcomers, whether because they have moved into the neighborhood, assisted-living facility or nursing home, or because they have come to inquire about belonging to our Church. The Roman Catholic Church and now some other major denominations need faithful elders to mentor in a formal way by participating in the Rite of Christian Initiation of Adults, the restored catechumenate. Every Christian denomination has its own way of incorporating new members into its community in Christ. Each community needs its elders to walk with the newcomers. If faith is a commitment to Christ, a growing attachment to and union with, who better to initiate the newcomer but one who has "walked the walk" for many decades?

We share wisdom among ourselves and with the next generation. We have probably grown simultaneously in compassion (of the heart) as we have been growing in wisdom (of the head) and grace (of the spirit). When we were younger perhaps we saw the world in all-or-nothing terms. Our faith and our morality may have been all or nothing too, without shades of gray. Our growth in faith, however, has led us to discover our own unique relationship with God/Jesus/Spirit. Growing in faith has led us to accept the paradoxes and mysteries of faith, even the sinfulness of Church leaders, without shock or disillusionment. We are now able to hold, as we begin to integrate the whole of our life, the whole of our faith with its seeming contradictions. We can nurture this multifaceted faith among our own age group, and encourage the generations behind us to question and search and then to share the fruits of their quest for God.

We may activate this gift of mature faith by leading adult faith-sharing or discussion groups in our Church community. We need not have answers for the questions of faith, but we can develop the ability to hear with an equanimity, a non-anxious presence, the feelings and doubts of the younger age group as they search for God. We know from long experience that the true teacher is the Holy Spirit if we can sit in silence and wait for the Spirit's light to reveal itself.

Gathering a group to share faith or study Scripture is a service to the community, a way to "wash feet" that calls upon our wisdom, all that the Spirit has been teaching us through our long years of listening. Other services may be more mundane, somewhat like the charity practiced by the widows of the early Church. They visited the sick and helped out the young mothers. They provided hospitality for travelers and were available in times of crises.

Suppose each local Church had a group of widows, widowers and older couples who could devote some of their retirement time to caring for the crisis situations that arise in the community. They might babysit during a young family's emergency, drive another elder to the doctor, sit silent with those in grief, bring communion to the sick and shut-ins, visit the homebound to read Scripture to them and listen to their stories, do a family's laundry when a parent is hospitalized.

This group of elders could gather each week or twice a month to pray together for those for whom they care, to encourage each other in tough situations, to back each other up, substitute if someone in the care-group will be away for a while. The pastor would be able to refer so many calls for pastoral care to this group of fruit-bearing volunteers.

They might train themselves through reading and discussing a book on pastoral ministry, or they might regularly call in resource people for training as they learn to be the pastoral care corps in the local Church. Stephen Ministry, most widespread in the Episcopal Church, is one form of preparation such a group might use. Some of the younger elders who read this book will be involved in this pastoral care of older elders, perhaps their own parents, aunts or uncles, which may be more difficult than service to the shut-ins of the parish. Dr. Lyon summarizes this vital ministry in the Church: "...pastoral care with the aging involves enabling older adults meaningfully and appropriately to care for and contribute to the lives of others even as it enables older adults meaningfully and appropriately to care for themselves" (*Toward a Practical Theology of Aging*, page 104).

While most pastors would welcome the support and the ministry of the community elders, fruit bearing need not be confined to building up the Church community. The dedication to building houses for the poor of former president Jimmy Carter and his wife Rosalyn after their sojourn among the rich and powerful of the world is a great witness to a fruitful aging. Eleanor Roosevelt, who used her widowhood so effectively for the lost and little ones of this world, wrote: "When you cease to make a contribution, you begin to die. I think it is a necessity to be doing something which you feel is helpful in order to grow old gracefully and attentively" (quoted in Fowler and McCutcheon, page 151).

Elders as Critics of Social Injustice

To make a prophetic contribution to society, one may either console or critique. The mission, the contribution can begin at home. To critique does not call us to be strident nor violent. Here is an example from an advertisement, "The Power of a Grandpa," almost a full-page ad in the *Washington Post*, January 26, 1999. The photo shows a child speaking to an older man, who leans toward him, intently listening.... The text, sponsored by the office of National Drug Control, reads:

> Children have a very special relationship with Grandma and Grandpa. That's why grandparents can be such powerful allies in helping keep a kid off drugs.

Grandparents are cool. Relaxed. They're not on the firing line every day. Some days a kid hates his folks. He never hates his grandparents. Grandparents ask direct, point-blank embarrassing questions you're too nervous to ask: "Who's the girl?" "How come you're doing poorly in history?" "Why are your eyes always red?" "Did you go to the doctor? What did he say?" The same kid who cons his parents is ashamed to lie to Grandpa. Without betraying their trust, a loving, understanding grandparent can discuss the danger of drugs openly with the child he adores. And should....As a grandparent you hold a special place in the hearts and minds of your grandchildren. Share your knowledge, your faith in them. Use your power as an influencer to steer your grandchildren away from drugs.

Whether homebound and on the telephone, whether healthy and active, we can take social and political action. For example, beginning and enlisting others in a letter-writing campaign, helping the voiceless get registered to vote, getting out the vote on election day, are ways to activate our prophetic gifts of critiquing the country's priorities. Elders healed of an overwhelming need for human respect can have a fierceness for justice, right speech and specific actions that will help "justice roll like a river" (Amos 5) through our country, state, county, town.

David Maitland observes: "...to my knowledge nobody [among gerontologists] sees older people as an informed source of social criticism. Our understanding of the services within their capability is largely limited to one-on-one care" (*Aging as Countercultural*, page 33).

Public figures like Dorothy Day, Mother Teresa of Calcutta and Pope John XXIII offered powerful social criticism in their eldest years. U.S. Congressman Claude Pepper worked tirelessly all through his old age for the causes of the elderly. Our friends Sister Catherine Pinkerton, C.S.J., and Sister Amata Miller, I.H.M., spent their older years working for Network, the Catholic Social Justice lobby in Washington, D.C.

Maitland personally knew a CEO of a large arms-producing

company in the United States who, after retirement, became chair of the Ford Foundation. This leader began to articulate "...hopes for a decrease in U.S. arms production so that the government can turn to the needs of single-parent families, homeless people and the rural poor." Once he had stepped away from a system that seemed to have given him his meaning, this man was gifted with a new and creative vision. Maitland notes that those still within the system have a hard time critiquing it, whereas in older age, we can shift from a focus on self to a focus on the healing of society (pages 37-38).

For Reflection and Prayer

Even if you are not retired, take a front page story today and spend fifteen minutes reading it, reflecting on it. Invite God to lend you God's own eyes and heart as you absorb the situation, the people involved. What do you feel? What do you want? Share these responses with God and listen for God to share with you.

With so much suffering in our world, in our own lives and the lives of those we love, we may be comforted by God's sharing these burdens with us. We are bearing fruit through it all.

As Saint Paul writes, through this mortal flesh of ours, beset on so many sides for so many years, we are letting the life of Christ shine through the earthen vessels that we are. More, in enfleshing Jesus in our own bodies, we are bearing the fruit of grace to ever more and more people:

> We carry such treasure in clay vessels so that it may be made clear that this extraordinary power belongs to God and does not come from us. We are afflicted in every way, but not crushed; perplexed, but not driven to despair; persecuted, but not forsaken; struck down, but not destroyed; always carrying in our body the death of Jesus so that the life of Jesus may also be made visible in our bodies.
>
> While we live we are always being given up to death for Jesus' sake that the life of Jesus may be made visible in our mortal flesh..... We know that the one who raised the Lord Jesus will raise us also with Jesus, and will bring us

with you into his presence. Yes, everything is for your sake, so that grace, as it extends to more and more people, may increase thanksgiving to the glory of God.
(2 Corinthians 4:7-15)

CHAPTER NINE

Pruning

"Every fruitful branch God prunes, that it might be more fruitful yet" (John 15:1). Pruning is God's work, another way that God tends us. In Jesus' Last Supper discourse, he names himself the vine and us the branches. He promises that when we have been fruitful God may well prune so that we, the branches, can bear more fruit. What is dead and decayed in us God will cut off so that new life might sprout in us and through us. The cutting process may be painful. God does not "will" any pain for its own sake. Often pain happens because we risk being fully human, fully alive, risk being who we are called to be.

Saint Paul is an example of one who did not seek suffering, and, in fact, begged God to remove the thorn from his flesh. But for the joy of preaching the Good News, he endured much pain and hardship. Paul, like Mary of Nazareth, is another New Testament person about whose aging we might surmise. He is a man who seems to age before our eyes as we read his letters in chronological order. He was a young man when he watched the stoning of Stephen, but old enough to have become a rabbi, with the trust of the Jewish leadership (Acts 7:59). Like many of us, he may have aged early from the sufferings he endured. He toiled night and day (1 Thessalonians 2:9) to support his mission work. In his travels under the most harsh and difficult conditions, in the torture meted out by his enemies, in his imprisonments in the cold, damp underground holes, in hunger and sleeplessness, he was weakened.

For Reflection and Prayer

Remember some things you have suffered over the course of your life. Write them down. What were the pains in your household growing up? What kind of adolescence did you have? What hardships did you feel as you "established" yourself, and perhaps a family of your own? If you work or worked outside your home, what injustices did you experience? When have you most deeply felt lonely, misunderstood, emotionally battered? Here is how the Lord Jesus comforted Paul, as Paul himself testifies: "The Lord said to me, 'My grace is made powerful in weakness.' Gladly would I rather boast of my weaknesses so that the power of Christ might overshadow. For the sake of Christ then, I am well pleased with weaknesses, insults, hardships, persecutions and difficulties, for when I am weak, then I am full of power" (2 Corinthians 12:9-10). What of Paul's experience—that in weakness the power of Christ, the Spirit of Christ, is strong—has been true in your life? Write down the specific incidents and feelings. What of Mary's growing weakness as she aged? Would Mary have experienced in her own mission work the insults, hardships, persecutions and weaknesses that Paul did? How do you think the power of Christ sustained her? Ask her. What are some of the specific weaknesses and insults that you have known just because you are getting older, more tired and frail year by year? Write them down. For example, confusion, memory lapses, falls, sleeplessness, shakiness in walking, difficulty in getting up from a deep chair (for Mary, from her bed on the floor). Have you ever been laughed at because of your weakness? Insulted? Ignored? Rushed, even by well-meaning younger friends? Share your memories and your feelings about it with Mary. Don't censor any memory or feeling, because you are completely safe with her. She understands even your bitterness and wants to comfort you with acceptance and eventual peace.

Suffering

There may indeed be pain ahead or there may not be. Most of us already know suffering firsthand. We have experienced it in childhood, in mid-life crises, in the loss of a loved one or our own self-ideal. We may be experiencing it right now in chronic illness, or in a relationship rift with adult sons or daughters, or in the lonesomeness of distance from our loved ones.

Suffering is different than pain. Pain, it seems, is the excruciating experience of an event—physical or emotional. Suffering is what follows. Pain and suffering are a part of every human life, but God's will is for our *shalom*, wholeness. Pain may be a part of our life from time to time, but according to Saint Ignatius of Loyola, the ordinary state of the Christian is meant to be consolation. Even in the midst of chronic physical pain, the key is in what meaning we make of our suffering. It may be an opportunity to be in union with the suffering body of Christ. Saint Paul wrote: "It makes me happy to suffer for you, as I am suffering now, and in my own body to do what I can to make up all that has still to be undergone by Christ for the sake of his body, the Church" (Colossians 1:24).

Jesuit philosopher and mystic Teilhard de Chardin wrote:

> Human suffering, the sum total of suffering poured out at each moment is like an immeasurable ocean. But what makes up this immensity? Is it blackness? Emptiness? Barren wastes? No indeed. It is the potential energy....
>
> [I]f all the sick people in the world were simultaneously to turn their sufferings into a single shared longing for the speedy completion of the kingdom of God, what a vast leap toward God the world would thereby make! (quoted in Finch, page 79)

Both Ignatian and Twelve-Step spirituality offer us an anchor in suffering, a remedy that has both a spiritual and a psychological base. It has been successful for the thousands who daily work the Twelve Steps of Alcoholics Anonymous and related groups. The first two steps proclaim: "We came to believe that we were powerless over _____, and that a power greater than ourselves wants to restore us to sanity." Yet many of us have invested much energy into pretending that we were perfectly sane and powerful. Some of us may have even worked diligently to ensure that there would be no power greater than ourselves, at least not on our floor or in our office or in our home. Thus it is most difficult to admit our creaturehood, our dependency.

Ignatius teaches us that the principle and foundation of spiritual growth is that God is our good Creator; that God has created every creature for our enjoyment, if only we recognize it as gift, not our right, not our entitlement. That spiritual base is to know in our bones, in our gut, that God is God and we are creatures. We are dependent, dependent on God, on others. We are born needy, and it is a lie, a denial of our creaturehood, our mortality, to pretend that we are entitled to any special consideration.

If we can let God rid us of a sense of entitlement, our anger and our suffering may become tempered. Our anguished "why" may be gentled into a "why not" as we live into the reality that indeed bad things do happen to good people, that no one of us is entitled to immunity from this painful experience.

Suffering is a mystery. It may come into our lives by chance—the car accident that robs us of a child, the tornado that devastates our town, the random acts of violence that seem to be growing in so many places, the physical illness that can strike us down, the Alzheimer's that robs us of our spouse. Or it may be the result of choices, our own or others', which can bring enormous pain into our lives; for example, the cutting off of a relationship because of differences or the deliberate choice of an unhealthy lifestyle.

The psychological base for our sanity (a word that in Latin means "healthy") is likewise the reality of knowing who we are. We are not God. As the psalmist bluntly puts it:

God knows how we are made,
God remembers that we are dust.
Our days pass like grass,
our prime like a flower in bloom.
A wind blows, the flower fades,
and its place is gone. (Psalm 103)

When we are put in our place as mere dust, paradoxically, we are gifted by God especially with the ability to think, to feel, to choose. When however our thinking is crooked, it can trigger inappropriate emotions, which sometimes lead to wrong, sinful and/or foolish choices. We unwittingly intensify our own suffering. Hopefully, even that pain will make the roots of all that God has planted in us deeper and stronger. "The works of God go forward slowly and painfully," wrote Blessed Mary Theresa Gerhardinger, S.S.N.D., "but the roots are all the deeper and the fruits all the lovelier." We are gradually learning that there is no rescue from being limited creatures, dependent and mortal, limited in many ways, gifted in so many other ways— not deserving, not entitled.

Suffering is a mystery, one that continues the passion of Christ. "We fill up what is wanting in the suffering of Christ" (Colossians 1:24). Like Jesus and Mary, we, too, have had sorrowful mysteries threading through our lives.

For Reflection and Prayer

Let us ponder yet again some of the pain, some of the sorrows and suffering in our life, asking God for the grace to see where it has strengthened our rootedness in Christ, shared in his passion, brought forth some fruit. List another, or the same, set of sorrowful mysteries of your own life. Ask the Spirit to call to mind what you need to know from exploring the depths of the sorrow once again. Then return to each mystery in turn and let the Spirit guide your journaling for an in-depth lesson about the depths of you.

The first remedy for suffering is to be convinced that God does not passionately desire, does not will, our suffering. Certainly suffering is not, as was once believed, a punishment for our sins and failures. We call on one of the most credible witnesses to God's love in our century, Mother Teresa of Calcutta:

> Suffering is not a punishment.
> God does not punish....
> Jesus does not punish.
> Suffering is a sign—a sign that we have come so close
> to Jesus on the cross
> that he can kiss us,
> show that he is in love with us,
> by giving us an opportunity to share in his passion.
> (quoted in Finch, page 80)

Oh, wondrous exchange! The embodiment of compassion, one beside whom even Mother Teresa's compassion fades, Jesus, offers us the chance to share suffering with him. The remedy for our suffering is gradually to accept every person, thing, event as a gift from God. The remedy for suffering is especially to accept our life with its joys, sorrows, pain and suffering. At some point, we may even be able to praise and thank God for everything in our life, joy and sorrow, even if we are not yet sure of the benefit of the pain and suffering.

To come to that point means mourning all that has not been, mourning the losses and disappointments in ourselves, in others, in life and God. Usually that means working it through, speaking of our suffering without judging it. We may speak with a trusted person, with ourself through journaling, with God through laying our hearts open to God in prayer. This process of grieving is a way of integrating, making whole, making sense of our life. May Sarton journaled about her deep fatigue after her stroke: "A pure June day. An early pale pink single peony is out and I picked two, and one velvety deep blue Siberian iris this afternoon. But it is a dismal afternoon inside me, so tired I am of never feeling well" (*After the Stroke*, page 64).

According to Erikson, integration is our last developmental task as human beings, usually begun around age sixty and lasting till we die. It is a spiritual process too, of forgiving others, ourself and God, whether we call it integration, *shalom* or reconciliation. Through Jesus' suffering all the scattered sufferings of our life are brought into a wholeness, are reconciled, accepted and made one.

Forgiveness

Part of reconciliation is forgiveness. We need to forgive ourselves, others and sometimes even God. Holding resentments and grudges takes precious energy that can be directed in more life-giving ways.

Kathleen Fischer points out four stages of forgiveness: "to forgo, leave it alone; to forbear, to abstain from punishing; to forget, to avert from memory; to refuse to dwell on the wrong; to forgive, to abandon the debt. To forgive and be forgiven both enables us to live and prepares us to die" (*Autumn Gospel*, page 129).

Abandoning debts, letting go what is owed to us in "righteousness," is an essential part of God's hope for human jubilee. The paradox is that until we are able to forgive, or at least to beg God for the gift of forgiving, we remain under the power of the person or event that has hurt us. Forgiveness, however, is not a simple act of the will. It, like all good things, is gift given freely and in God's good time by the Giver of all gifts, God.

For Reflection and Prayer

Take some time now to think of persons you need to forgive and write down their names. Hold this list in your hand in a prayer gesture of openness to God. If you can't think of any one person, is there a group whom you resent? If there is no one or no group blocking you, ask the Spirit to "probe you and know your heart" (Psalm 139), and to bring to light any situation which you may have buried, suppressed. Ask the Spirit to help you write freely and truthfully about the hurt that is binding you. Hold what you have written as a prayer-offering. Ask God for the gift of forgiveness when God sees you are ready.

Forgiveness begins at home. In the exercise above, did you list your own name? We need to be able to embrace our own selves and to forgive the ways we have sinned against ourselves by making poor choices or neglecting life-giving ones. The gift of accepting forgiveness for our own mistakes is no less important than extending forgiveness to family, friends, even God, when we experience hurt or betrayal. In an article, "The Sacrament of Time," Kristen Johnson Ingram writes of the time of her elderly mother's dying. It was a call to forgiveness. "My mother's time was ripe and overripe, spoiled, because she and I spent so much of it angry or with our feelings hurt" (page 30). How important to forgive and be forgiven, to reconcile before coma or sudden death snatches our loved one away.

Diminishment

Sometimes our pruning is swift and sharp. Often it is the long, stripping process that Jesuit Pierre Teilhard de Chardin reflected on in his old age, what he termed "the passivities of diminishment" (*The Divine Milieu*, page 52). There have been the passivities of pruning even during our early life: the untimely death of a loved one, the loss of a child to death or to drugs, the displacement from a homeland, injustice in various forms.

Humanly speaking, the internal passivities of diminishment

> ...form the blackest residue and most despairingly useless years of our life. Some were waiting to pounce on us as we first awoke: natural failings, physical defects, intellectual or moral limitations, as a result of which the field of our activities, of our enjoyment, of our vision, has been ruthlessly limited since birth. Others were lying in wait for us later on and appeared as suddenly and brutally as an accident, or as stealthy as an illness. (*The Divine Milieu*, page 54)

The distinction between the frail and the healthy elderly is often made like a stroke of the sword. One day we are in fine spirits and good health. The next, after heart attack, car accident, great grief, serious fall, stroke, we are diminished drastically. May Sarton expresses this in *After the Stroke*: "And I felt so safe and well. Now I've been knocked down—and that is what is difficult—to be suddenly old—to foresee canceling all public appearances. A radical change of life" (page 44).

The psalmist knew this anguish as well:

> When I think: I have lost my foothold,
> your mercy, Love, holds me up.
> When cares increase in my heart,
> your consolation calms my heart. (Psalm 94)

Depression

Sometimes depression prevents us from looking at our life with compassion. One of the pains of depression is being burdened with guilt, usually far in excess of whatever real faults or omissions may exist. Fortunately at this time in history great progress has been made in treating this debilitating illness. New, focused cognitive therapeutic techniques and effective medications are available. So, if we find ourselves really stuck in a morass of guilt and an inability to forgive ourselves, we may be wise to talk to our physician about depression.

A sixty-nine-year-old woman, Margaret, who was very devoted to her sister, found her own life turned upside down in the year following the sudden death of her brother-in-law, which occurred suddenly while the two couples were vacationing. Margaret wanted to be available for her grieving sister and frequently included her in dinner invitations and outings. She saw her sister daily. But her sister, somewhat controlling and demanding, started taking out all the anger about her husband's death on her sister, accusing Margaret of selfishness and wanting to live her own life. If Margaret's plans did not meet Joan's expectations, Joan would lash out with anger and criticism.

Margaret started losing sleep, worrying that indeed she wasn't doing enough, that she was being selfish in her desire to reclaim some of her own life with her husband. A deeply religious woman, she sincerely wanted to love her sister in a practical way and to help her get through these grueling, grieving first months of widowhood. By the time Margaret sought some help, however, she had fallen down the slippery slope of depression, losing sleep and appetite, unable to think clearly, unable to enjoy the many interests that had normally brightened her life since retirement.

Probably most debilitating was the increasingly strong conviction that she was not a good person, that somehow in real and unforgivable ways she was letting her sister down by not being able to take her pain away and by not being totally available to her. A very brief stint of counseling coupled with a mild dose of antidepressant medicine helped to restore balance to her thinking and to her life. She continued to be a great support to her sister but changed some of her own debilitating, de-selfing behavior. She established some healthy boundaries in her own life. Most importantly, the heavy burden of unrealistic guilt lifted as she became more able to think clearly and realistically about some of the unrealistic "oughts" and "shoulds" that she had embraced.

Sometimes our "senior moments" frighten us as young elders. Are we slipping into senility? Stress, sleep deprivation, sugar imbalances, depression—all can cause us to lose concentration. Dementia is diagnosed when not only memory but at least one other cognitive disturbance is present. Some of those cognitive malfunctions, problems with thinking, include not only loss of memory, but losing words; a decline in ability to make decisions; difficulty in learning new information, difficulty with attention and concentration; difficulties in communicating or receiving communication. Some of those cognitive problems are also symptoms of depression. Thus the difficulty. Let us briefly attend to Alzhheimer's disease, delirium and dementia before returning to the topic of depression.

We don't really know what Alzheimer's disease means, but we can tell with CT (CAT) scans and PT (PET) scans, two different ways of imaging the brain, when there has been a "vascular accident," a stroke, or shock as it is called in New England. TIA (transient ischemic accident; a mini-stroke) patients gradually or even quickly return to full functioning, as do many stroke patients with rehabilitation. Dr. Bill Long, a psychologist who specializes in gerontology, insists that we don't limit the CVA (cardio-vascular accident) patient, because they could come back. They may be prone to crying or cursing, usually some different emotional response kept long repressed, but Long urges us to keep working with them. May Sarton certainly struggled back from her stroke: "I have been in that same state of 'not being able'—and the frustration and depression it causes. I was tired I think—at any rate I found I was stumbling over words in a strange way—substituting one word for another. That is surely an effect of the stroke" (*After the Stroke*, page 147).

Delirium, especially in the frail elderly, can be particularly frightening, but most easily helped. It usually stems from infection or toxic imbalance of medications. Delirium is a perceptual disorder sometimes brought on either by sensory deprivation or by overstimulation. It mimics depression at times because of our decreased attention span, lower level of consciousness and slowed psychomotor activity. Disorganized thinking, altered sleep/wake cycles, disorientation and memory impairment are other symptoms. Sometimes alcoholism kept secret can look like delirium. Delirium can develop quickly, sometimes within hours. This physical, toxic insult to our brain can be caused by stress of any type: stroke, fever, urinary tract infection, head trauma, any infection. The first treatment is of the underlying cause and sometimes, the weaning off medications, all, of course, under a physician's care.

Those with dementia are also likely to be depressed, not only because of loss, but because dementia affects the lower brain center and physiological changes occur. For those of us who care for the frail elderly, it is important to understand and counteract a mistaken diagnosis of dementia when the person is really suffering from depression. Dr. Long claims that if we were to treat the whole elderly population in the United States for depression, fifty percent of the so-called "demented" would be healed.

True dementia in one we love is agonizing. We might need to learn how to communicate in a totally different way with our loved one if language abilities decline. We might need to find a nursing home. Those with dementia do have lucid periods, and in fact, Dr. Long suggests that while the person still has days of clear thinking, it will be easier for them to adjust to the routine of the nursing facility. People can be aware that they are demented. They can take small bites of reality, although the size of their working memory is reduced. Poet Dorothy Anne Cahill, C.S.C., as bright as ever at eighty-four, images these bites of reality in the poem "Tempus":

Time was,
Tearing with strong teeth
Great chunks of time,
Stewing in careless superfluity
Minutes and days,

I let fall
So many priceless hours
From the platter of my living.
Now with precious care
I nibble the edges
Of moments,
Savoring each crumb,
Treasuring the taste of life
Against my larder's
Dwindling supply.

We who care for the frail elderly can tailor their environment so they can manage it. In their lucid periods, we can engage our demented loved ones in decisions about their own life.

Depression in the elderly often causes somatic complaints rather than psychological symptoms. For example, recovery from surgery for a broken hip means getting the anesthesia out of our system, as well as a rehabilitation program usually outside our home. Both anesthesia and separation can lead to depression, and therefore we might not cooperate with rehab therapists and the medications regimen. So, we are transferred to a long-term care facility. That is the aftermath of a broken hip. The results from stroke are worse.

Pity me, God, for I have no strength left.
Heal me, my bones are in torment.
...set me free because you love me...
I am worn out with groaning. (Psalm 6:2, 4, 6)

We are susceptible, at any age, to the apathy, withdrawal and loss of self-esteem that are symptoms of depression. Major depression, however, meaning that symptoms are present every day for at least two weeks, at any time of life, makes us more susceptible to depression in old age. Sometimes we can become depressed over the aging process itself. Betty Friedan, whose writing portrays such optimism, herself dreaded her sixtieth birthday. Thus we write, and you read, a book like this. Thus we all pray: Holy Spirit, don't let me deny truth today. Some Christian seniors fiercely deny they are depressed, cannot even admit that they "feel bad." Their early training makes them afraid of complaining, of being a burden to anyone. Yet they cannot concentrate and so, without understanding themselves and without treatment, they can begin to lose their memory and other cognitive functions.

For Reflection and Prayer

Let us take some time to pray with the psalmist and with all those who suffer these bodily, mental, and emotional pains:

> You saw me suffer, Love, you know my pain...
> Pity me, Lord, I hurt all over.
> My eyes are swollen, my heart and body ache.
> Grief consumes my life, sighs fill my days;
> Guilt saps my strength, my bones dissolve....
> Forgotten like the dead, I am a shattered jar. (Psalm 31)

> My days dissolve like smoke,
> my bones are burned to ash.
> My heart withers away like grass.
> I even forget to eat,
> so consumed am I with grief.
> My skin hangs on my bones.
> My days pass into evening,
> I wither like grass.
> Yet your servants...cherish even the rubble. (Psalm 102)

We not only cherish "the rubble," but we hope to treat it, to rebuild it. Thirty percent of all frail elderly are diagnosed as depressed. Ninety percent of that thirty percent experiences clinical depression. In this population, clinical depression is often associated with a medical problem. For example, depression exacerbates pain, calls for more use of health care services, longer hospital stays, longer rehabilitation, and can sometimes even lead to suicide. Because depression is so easily treated both by psychotherapy and medication, it is well to offer both to those who need it. For those who are simply waiting to die, who suffer from a lack of pleasure, a disconnection, an extreme lassitude, psychotherapy can be very useful. This "talk therapy" can be especially helpful in rebuilding self-esteem. Cognitive therapy, the straightening out of "crooked thinking," for example, all-or-nothing thinking, catastrophizing, or using a negative filter, can also work well. Yet, as Dr. Long cautions, it may take twice as long to do the therapy.

We believe that some older elders may need to learn how to use their therapists, however. Two stories reveal this. The first is of Pat whose daughter asked his physician to prescribe a counselor for his progressive depression. After the first session, Pat called his daughter to say his counselor told him to divorce his wife right away and move to a senior retirement community. This man was probably so debilitated by his newly uncovered dependence that he was looking for someone to tell him how to live his life. Pat misunderstood, and then clung to what was probably the counselor's open-ended question to him about possible options. The second story is of Gigi, a sprightly but frail elder whose daughter likewise wanted her to see a therapist. The therapist duly visited Gigi every week in the nursing home. Gigi told us, "It's difficult to think up each week some stories to amuse this nice young man." So used to being hospitable, Gigi had reversed their roles.

For Reflection and Prayer

If anxiety is present a simple remedy is to breathe from the diaphragm. Try this simple exercise. Place your hands on your stomach and try to breathe by only moving the chest. Then put your hands on your stomach and chest. Notice what happens. Then breathe only moving your stomach. Notice the difference that deep diaphragmatic breathing makes. This kind of deep breathing is often easier to learn and practice than some of the other relaxation techniques. The Spirit is called the breath of God. Breathe in deeply of God's Spirit, the Spirit of peace, the Spirit who is God's love.

As we ourselves age we may also be a caregiver for an aging, demented and/or dying spouse or sibling. We need a support system at once. With family often scattered around the country, we may need to ask friends, local church groups, and neighbors, as well as extended family, to spell us. We need to learn about whatever disease afflicts our loved one and what is to come, for example, incontinence. Along with our grief, we may expect to feel a whole gamut of emotion: anger, resentment, guilt and a depression of our own. "To be angry with her is so unreasonable," one man cried, "because her illness isn't her fault!" Exactly! Emotions are not reasonable. They are part of our wholeness, and they need to be expressed—to God, to a friend outside the situation, a minister, a therapist.

Throwing Ourselves on the Mercy of God

Some Christians are still afraid of God's judgment at the time of their death. They see their suffering on earth as punishment instead of pruning. While many are afraid of the process of dying, some are afraid of hell. Here is more good news as God harvests us home, from a very credible source. Jesus told a parable about the generosity and mercy of God, especially at the last minute. Like the prodigal son parable, this one rankles many long-term, hard-working, trying-to-be-perfect Christians. It is the story of the vineyard owner who goes out at break of day to hire laborers to work in his vineyard. They agree to work for the going wage. At different periods throughout the day, the vineyard owner returns to the town square and whoever he finds there still without work, he hires and sends them into his vineyard. At the last hour, the owner finds a few not yet hired. When it is time to pay his workers, beginning with those who worked only an hour, the owner hands them a full day's wage. The first ones hired smile in anticipation of a large increase by the time their turn comes. Not so. When they complain that they have borne the heat of the day, the owner asks them: "Did we not agree to the usual wage? Or are you jealous that I am generous?" (Matthew 20:1-15)

We are those "last hour workers." Even if we have borne the heat of the day, we are still "unprofitable servants," and blessed by the mercy and generosity of the Master. Pope John XXIII named himself a miserable sinner, as he prayed to die well: "Such life as remains to me shall not be anything other than a calm and happy preparation for death. I accept him and await him in faith and trust. I trust not in myself, for I am a miserable sinner, but in the boundless mercy of the Lord, whom I have to thank for everything I am and have" (from Finch, page 98).

Dom Helder Camara, the charismatic bishop of Brazil, noted not only for his charity but for his unusually courageous stands for social justice, also reflected on mercy at our last hour:

> As one approaches death, one is greatly tempted to add up one's shortcomings, weaknesses and sins, and to lose courage. I believe it is better not to count at all, not to debate at all. Yes, my shortcomings, weaknesses and sins are even more numerous and graver! But there is that which is even greater than my shortcomings, weaknesses and sins—the mercy of the Lord! Some day the sun will set for each of us for the last time. Sister light, would it be possible to warn me when my last day dawns? But best of all is still the endeavor of the Christian to live each day as if it were the last: or better still—as if it were ever the first. (quoted in Finch, page 100)

The blessing of old age is that we can with more trust than ever throw ourselves on the mercy of God. God's generosity is not a kind of reward. Instead, the good news is that even in the midst of hardship, loss, disease that "...God suffers with us in our hardship, loss, or disease, and offers us a blessing. God suffers with the victim of Alzheimer's disease, with the destitute aged of our great cities...God suffers with us and offers us blessing—the power of life in the face of death" (Lyon, page 115).

The MacArthur Foundation researchers concluded that successful aging involved the ability to maintain three key behaviors or characteristics:

- low risk of disease and disease-related disability
- high mental and physical function
- active engagement with life. (*Successful Aging*, page 38)

We conclude that successful aging, even if disease, disability, malfunctioning of our bodies or physical isolation diminish us, includes these key characteristics:

- acceptance of our one and only life just as it is
- receptivity to all that God wants to lavish
- growing union with the suffering and rising of Christ
- willingness to admit and accept that indeed, the Master is merciful and generous!

The fruitful branch, the person open to and cooperative with God's pruning, has certainly aged well.

CHAPTER TEN

Harvesting

L ord, bring us back
as water to thirsty land.
Those sowing in tears
reap, singing and laughing.

They left weeping, weeping,
casting the seed.
They come back, singing, singing,
holding high the harvest. (Psalm 126)

Gathering the Harvest of Our Lives

To harvest means to cut down. We begin in tears and end in
singing. We are pruned, but we are fulfilled. Polly Francis,
international fashion photographer and essayist, wrote in her
nineties about this process:

> Age creeps up so stealthily that it is often with shock that
> we become aware of its presence. Perhaps that is why so
> many of us reach old age utterly unprepared to meet its
> demands. We may be a bit rebellious about accepting it; I
> want to cry out that the invisible part of me is not old, I
> still thrill to the beauties of this world—the dew upon the
> rose at dawn, the glow reflected by the sun on a passing
> cloud when day is done—but unremitting age goes on.
>   My interest in the goings-on in the world outside my
> ever-tightening barriers has not been withdrawn. It is not
> interest I have lost, but rather the means of getting around
> and the physical stamina to sustain me as I go. It is my
> task now to build a new life ("The Autumn of My Life,"
> quoted in Fowler and McCutcheon, page 31).

Kathleen Fischer in *Autumn Gospel* says about the gathering in of the harvest: "All that we have been and done continues to live on as part of us. Our history dwells in our whole being" (page 123). The central mystery of our Christian faith is that all of Christ's dying and rising lives on as part of us. This Christ-mystery is based on the reality of dynamic memory. In the Eucharist we remember and give thanks and make real again the kernel of the Good News, the paschal mystery that "Christ has died. Christ is risen. Christ will come again." By God's awesome and continuing gift of the incarnation, Christ remains alive in us, suffers, dies and rises in each one of our lives. Remembering and giving thanks is central to being Christian. It is central to the human task of harvesting our lives.

In her book *Gold in Our Memories*, Macrina Wiederkehr, O.S.B., offers a poetic and passionate glimpse of ways in which we encounter the sacred in our own memories. Each one of us carries in our hearts the archives of our one and only life. One of the tasks as we grow older is to mine this gold in our memories, to sift and sort and let the light of the Son reveal the redemption in our lives. We need to sort out the stories of joy and savor again the memories of kindnesses given and returned. We need to return to the painful places also, to look again for the blessing. We need to forgive, ourselves and others, so that the energy we use to hold resentments and grudges can be directed in more life-giving ways.

Stories

There are many ways to reconstruct the story of our lives, not just for ourselves but also for the gift that it can be to others. In her practical little book *The Mystery of My Story*, Paula Sullivan reminds us that "every person is an unfinished story. By writing down the stories accumulated as we journey through life, we begin to recognize some of the paradoxes, both human and divine, and step into the mystery of 'the religious way'"(page 5).

How do we begin to create this memory patchwork quilt of our own story? We can tell the story chronologically or we can tell our stories in a more free-flowing journaling exercise. Here is an example how one of our respondents experimented with trying to compose a memory picture while pondering Macrina Wiederkehr's *Gold in Our Memories*. Note both the spontaneity of the memory and the feelings it allowed to bubble up—truly an experience of being surprised by joy.

The first time I tried to do this exercise happened at a most surprising place. I, who hate to fly, had been dropped at Baltimore's airport several hours before my flight. It was early morning, and while the main corridors of the terminal were bustling with activity the observation deck was relatively empty and quiet. A warm November sun brought light and warmth and comfort. In one of the easy chairs of the deck I settled down to read, to muse with this lovely book. Only God knows why the first thing that popped out of my heart-memory was my godson, Brian. Perhaps it was the very recent memory of seeing him with his sister's firstborn. His look of tender delight rivaled the way the baby's Daddy looked at her—full of love, awe, absorbed delight in this beautiful new creation called Catie. Whatever the reason, sitting there at B.W.I. airport, the image that came to me was Brian, age four, and what still more than twenty years later, remains one of the happiest memories of my life.

To celebrate his fourth birthday his parents let me take him to a child's amusement park outside of Baltimore appropriately called Enchanted Forest. This was a child's park, pre-hi-tech, pre-thrill, relying solely on a child's capacity for wonder, kiddie-sized rides, kiddie-style space for wonder and imagination riding through the "Jungle," "Wonderland," bouncing in a "moonland" made of rubber balls.

Somehow that day, that experience became an icon of the multiple occasions of joy and delight that Brian, his siblings, and his cousins have been for me who have no children of my own. That day in the airport I wrote the following haiku and hope to begin the practice of writing picture haikus for each of these now grown children. I watch them delight in their own nieces and nephews as I once did, and still do, in them.

Enchanting four
Enchanted Forest
Heart-cheering godson.
Color him gift.

One of the ways that Weiderkehr suggests that we can mine the gold in our memories is by trying to write a haiku (a seventeen-syllable poem) to capture our experience. It's easier than it sounds!

For Reflection and Prayer

Take a few minutes now to let some joyful memory in your life bubble to the surface. Spend some time writing about it with as much freedom as you can. Don't worry about "good form"—just let your writing flow. Try then to take what you have written and capture its kernel in a haiku if you can.

There are many simple techniques that we can use in trying to write our story.

Writing our story is not necessarily the same as writing history. Personal memory has its own unique lens. In writing our own reality we color the experience with personal feeling and energy. One way to start might be by simply listing people in our lives who have been important. Then next to each name we can jot some phrases and descriptions that evoke the person, and some of the experiences that we have shared.

It is amazing how nuanced memory can be. In an interview with two elderly sisters they recalled the same aunt. They both used similar adjectives, but note the subtle differences as one described her aunt as "frugal, thrifty, and careful," while the other described this same woman as "stingy and tight." Same person being remembered, same essential description, but modulated through the lens of individual memory.

Writing Our Own Story

Another way to harvest memories is simply to address the basic journalistic questions—who? when? where? how? why?—to the particular memory that we are writing about. Another is to look back at our own life in terms of choices that we have made, roles that we have lived into. Most of us have lived both simultaneously and successively a number of roles—daughter, son, sister, brother, wife, husband, mother, father, colleague, member of ___, professional person. As we do this healing exercise of naming and claiming our many roles we also may be preparing a legacy for the persons who will follow us. As we grow older we often are graced with new perspectives, a new sense of acceptance. What may have puzzled or frazzled or frustrated us in the past may become understood in a new way.

Photos can also enable this process. In fact there is a whole powerful school of therapy called phototherapy that facilitates healing through interaction with photos. The client tells her or his story by creating a collage, choosing from a lifetime of photos the twenty or so that capture the most personal story.

However old we are there is in our memory bank the recollection of those older than we. These persons who live in our heart may represent how we would like to age, or perhaps there are others whose memory is less positive. Let us remember some of those men and women who have aged well, or at least the best they could. Perhaps these are persons to whom we pray regularly, our pioneers who have preceded us in death as well as life. We may have pictures of these folks, if not actual photos, at least pictures in the album of our hearts.

For Reflection and Prayer

Ponder these photos, or graphic memories in your heart. You may want to write about them, what further memories they evoke and what feelings arise in you.

Here is an example from Rachel's own life:

> Right now I am looking at a picture of my eighty-one-year-old uncle. He is holding his youngest granddaughter, not quite four. His eyes are twinkling with delight and punctuate Grampie's face with warmth and joy. His large hands are knotted with arthritis and his broad Irish face is

lined with crinkly smile lines. He is sitting at his daughter's family-room table with paperwork spread out in front of him. But he has taken off his glasses and is visibly enjoying the interruption by his youngest grandchild.

I can practically hear both of them giggling. He's gotten a little hard of hearing and his eyesight isn't as good as it was, but he is still practicing law out of his home and actively shuttling his wife to meetings, hairdresser, grandchildren, friends. He loves his Boston Red Sox with that kind of wacky loyalty that seems peculiar to Bosox fans. Being around him is like being near a wood stove on a cold day. His humor, his interest, his delight in life, especially surprises, is life-giving. He adores his grandchildren, by now twelve in number. He still goes out to toss a football with his seven-year-old grandson, much to his wife's chagrin. "Grampie, bring lots of breath!" Brendan calls as the game begins.

A participant at daily Mass, his faith is lived more than preached. He and his wife say the beads daily at the end of the day—audibly, at a breakneck speed that only the Lord can decipher. Yet, there is no doubt how much this good man who has lived a full but in some ways very ordinary life is beloved by God.

This photo I am contemplating was taken a few months before he suffered a ruptured aortic aneurysm, an aneurysm he had known about for a couple of months. He was gambling that it would hold beyond the golden wedding anniversary celebration that was in the planning. It was typical of him that when the aneurysm finally ruptured, he walked out of his home to the ambulance. It was also typical that in his typewriter was a half-finished piece of business and in his desk drawer a number of stamped envelopes with dates penciled in when they should be sent.

He died a couple of days after his surgery. There is no doubt that had he recovered, this illness would have been a life-changing event. Sometimes I wonder how he would have dealt with being an invalid. As a friend wrote after he died, "He lived until he died"—probably the most fervent wish that any of us have.

Let me share another picture. This is a photo of his wife, Ruth, likewise taken only a few months before her death. She is, as always, dressed to kill. Her deep purple suit is set off by a stylish scarf that somewhat hides the severity of her osteoporosis slump. Her face is thinner than it has ever been. There is a deep haunting sadness in her eyes even as she is mustering a big smile for the camera. Their twinkle has never been the same since the death of her beloved John. Her hands are gripped in a familiar hand-wringing position which always gives away her nervousness. She loves her grandchildren but is not able to relish how very much her beloved John lives on in each of them in distinct and delightful ways. Worry overtakes her too often and it shows in this picture.

There is a part of Ruth that has never recovered from her own mother's death during the 1918 flu epidemic. She was twelve at the time, down with the flu herself and not even told about her mother's death until her own recovery a week after the funeral. As she has aged, her frequent return to this pain signals how unfinished it is for her and helps me to understand a little better her chronic anxiety and her sometimes erratic moods, which age and debility have worsened.

With unstinting devotion from her daughter at home for a number of years, she managed to soldier on in her own beautiful home, still filled with traces of John. But her own diminishing health has made it impossible for her to remain at home alone. Now as this picture is taken she has moved into the home of her other daughter, equally devoted. By now Ruth is suffering a great deal of pain from, as she called it, "the osteo thing."

In this photo, Ruth still shows an impish sense of humor. More frequently now it is marred by her querulous frustration at some of her limitations, forgetfulness, pain, acute homesickness for her home and her adult children hours away. She is happiest with company, especially with people who, like herself, can gently tease. Her generosity never diminishes. Nothing delights her more than giving presents. A leisurely morning rosary has replaced daily Mass, but she is still able to get out for ice cream and other rides. However, she has shrunk so much that her head is barely up to the car window. Her daughter, who has many of John's life-giving qualities, energy and optimism, is ingenious at thinking of ways to get Ruth out despite her frailty.

I, who share more of Ruth's timidity, am more fearful of these excursions but do treasure our last trip to the National Arboretum in spring. Ruth's charm and her joy in the beauty of the azaleas banking the hillsides there is a cherished and life-giving memory for me.

Ruth's final illness was very difficult. She experienced increasing breathing difficulties which made her more anxious and panicky. It culminated in the bacterial pneumonia which made her delirious and killed her. The night before she died, in her delirium she went from room to room in her own home, mentally drawing the blinds and turning off the lights, a poignant metaphor for us of her good-bye to the hearth of her life.

Since she has died I have prayed to her and felt her presence very closely. She has replaced Saint Anthony for me as my finder of lost things. She has never failed! I think that our good God has let me know for sure that Ruth is in heaven and that all is well, despite worry and snappishness (hers and mine!).

While I would so wish to have the courage and zest for life that my uncle enjoyed I know that my "Callahan genes" shared with Ruth have left me timid and anxious and too often afraid to go that extra mile. But it's the best that I can do, and Ruth continually reminds me that's OK. God's grace and goodness work in us in our quirkiness as well as in our gifts.

"Glory be to God whose power at work in us can do infinitely more than we can ask or imagine" (Ephesians 3:20).

For Reflection and Prayer

Take some time to thumb through your own heart album. Whose pictures do you see? What stories do they hold for you? How do they give you food for this part of your journey?

Legacies

What is it in our lives that we would like to pass on? We might reflect about what we want to give to the next generation. Certainly, the stories. While they may be written out, it is especially precious to the younger generation to have our voices captured on audiotape as we tell our family history. Videotape is even a greater consolation to those we leave behind. Even in ancient days, the psalmist knew how important it was to "recount" God's wonders in our lives.

> You are my shelter...my rock and haven,...my tower
>   of strength.
> ...You keep me in your care...
> Now I am old, my strength fails. Do not toss me aside.
> Do not leave me, Lord, now that I am old.
> I can still recount to a new generation your power and
>   strength. (Psalm 71)

One of our legacies as we get older might be the gift of having set our affairs in order. There are many practical handbooks about what is involved in "getting our affairs in order"— making a will, for example, including the living will and durable power of attorney that will protect ourselves and our loved ones from undesired medical interventions. Some choose to leave the legacy of their bodies to science. Rea carries an organ donor card, thinking should she die prematurely, perhaps one of her healthy fifty-seven-year-old lungs might help another fifty-seven-year-old who needs a lung transplant.

Even if our body is donated to a medical school, our family needs a memorial service. Making our own funeral arrangements, and especially the more personal planning of our own wake service and funeral liturgy, can be a way of befriending our own mortality as well as sparing loved ones from having to deal with those practicalities at the time of our death. Choosing special hymns and favorite Scriptures for the funeral is a way to continue to share our faith with loved ones.

These, however, are not the only legacies on which we want to focus. Let us also look at some of those less tangible legacies, the wisdom, the stories that have nourished us and that we want to transcend our physical lives. Generativity is a powerful human need, the desire to participate in something beyond ourselves, something that will live longer than we will. Many live out this generativity in their parenting and grandparenting roles and other caregiving roles. In a previous chapter we looked at some of the ways that elders can be generative in the community.

Now let us focus on the close relationships, how we are generative among family and friends. Generativity saves us from the life-sapping preoccupation of self-absorption. Anthropologist Margaret Mead notes: "From grandparents children learn to understand something about the reality of the world not only before they were born but also before their parents were born... Experience of the past gives them means of imaging the future" (quoted in Fowler and McCutcheon, page 201).

For Reflection and Prayer

Reflect upon what you would like to pass on. What bits of wisdom, your own or ones you have received? Are there stories of the generations before you that you need to hand on?

Legacies take many shapes and forms. One mother chose as the first sentence of her will: "To my beloved children, my first and dearest gift to them is the gift of Faith." Mrs. Murphy wanted to make explicit what she had lived. This single mother of three, suddenly widowed in midlife, had drawn much strength and comfort from the practice of her faith and very much wanted to pass it on.

As we grow older we become the keepers of "far memory." We are the ones who were there—at Pearl Harbor (or at least hunched over the radio for news of it), during the Civil Rights movement, when the first human being set foot on the moon. While the technology of this century has captured the sights and sounds of these moments, it is the living memory which carries the stories. We bear the "far memory" of the day our adult sons and daughters were born. We are the ones who can keep alive for the next generations the stories of the last generation and of our own.

Gathering In

Erikson reminds us that the primary developmental task of this part of our lives is integration. As we gather the story of our life we seek to find its meaning, to come to an acceptance of its many twists and turns. In *The Divine Milieu*, Pierre Teilhard de Chardin reflects upon what he calls "the passivities of diminishment" (page 52). These are all those external and internal events that happen to us. Each life is marked with all the incidents and accidents, small or monumentally large, which forever change the landscape of our lives. Is one lifetime long enough to reconcile the tragedy of an untimely death? the loss of a child? the exodus of displacement from a homeland? The challenge of this period of our life is to come to grips with that greatest of paradoxes: "Unless a grain of wheat fall into the ground and die it remains alone. But if it dies it brings forth much fruit" (John 12:24).

All life contains the seeds of its own death, and death in turn can nourish new life. Perhaps at no other period of our lives is this dance between life as ascent (becoming more fully ourselves) and life as descent (letting go and diminishment) more poignant and pronounced. If we can do this dance with as much awareness as we are capable of, we will be ready for that moment when our good God comes to harvest us home.

We are waiting, but not in anxiety nor depressed. As the psalmist writes: "At daybreak you listen for my voice, Love. At dawn I hold myself in readiness for you. I watch for you" (Psalm 5:3).

In *Anam Cara*, his book on Celtic spirituality, John O'Donohue writes of how the Irish see death as a wound in the world, and yet one leading to new birth. He describes this final waiting which eventually leads to death as both a gathering in and a deep longing:

> ...always waiting for the great moment of gathering or belonging, and it always evades us. We are haunted with a

deep sense of absence. There is something missing from our lives. We always expect it to be filled by a definite person, object, or project. We are desperate to fill this emptiness, but...this absence can never be filled. (page 222)

Conscious Dying

Many of us have been taught to pray for the grace of a happy death. We repeat this prayer every time we say a Hail Mary, asking Mary to "pray for us now, and at the hour of our death." Yet, we each have our own idea of what constitutes a happy death. However we dream about or dread its particulars, a "happy death" means that indeed God has harvested us home. The great good news of our Christian faith is that by his life, death and resurrection, Jesus has forever transformed death into life. "Death is the sum and consummation of all our diminishments." (de Chardin, *The Divine Milieu*, page 54). But we believe that "Christ has conquered death." As Saint Thérèse of Lisieux asserted: "It is not death that will come for me, but God."

Finishing Well

How can we embrace this reality, especially in a culture which is so phobic about death? By this time of our lives most of us have been present at somebody's death: parent, sibling, friend or, unthinkably, even our child. Unless the death has been sudden we may have been able to participate in our loved one's "finishing well." *Tuesdays with Morrie* is a moving chronicle of "finishing well." Morrie, a university professor who had lived to the hilt, literally dancing through life, was stricken with Lou Gehrig's disease. ALS gradually stripped him of all motor capacity. One of his former students, established as a journalist, saw Morrie in a television interview and returned to sit once more not at the feet of his mentor, but at his bedside. In their regular Tuesday meetings Morrie showed rather than told his student about dying well. Morrie's capacity for gratitude enlarged as his physical capacities waned. His freedom in the face of this ravaging, death-dealing disease grew even as his dependence upon others for the most basic needs escalated. Life is to be savored, however tiny the sip.

For Reflection and Prayer

Who has been a "Morrie" for you? What did he/she teach you about finishing well?

Another example of finishing well was reported by a middle-aged woman who had just lost her mother. Conscious that she was getting closer to death Mrs. G. used some of her rapidly failing energy to tell her adult sons and daughters very explicitly that they had been good sons and daughters to her, that she was grateful and how much she loved each one of them. What a gift, especially to the ones who were not so sure that they had been good children. What a final blessing!

For Reflection and Prayer

What is your idea of finishing well? Who would you like to be with you? Who/what are you grateful for? Think about the final blessing that you would like to give.

Here is the blessing for the dying with which John O'Donohoe concludes his book on Celtic friendship, *Anam Cara*:

A Blessing for Death

...May there be a beautiful welcome for you in the home that you are going to...going back to the home that you never left.
May you have a wonderful urgency to live your life to the full...
May your going be sheltered and your welcome assured.
May your soul smile in the embrace of your *anam cara*.
(pages 230-31)

For Reflection and Prayer

Write your final blessing out for your memorial service or funeral liturgy. Remember all those who will gather to remember you and wish them, bless them with all that you know they will need in their grief.

Wheat, Gathered to One

An ancient Church document, *The Didache*, speaks of grain scattered on the hillside, yet brought together into one loaf. So are we gathered, brought into unity within ourselves, into unity with one another. We are gifted with *shalom*, meaning integration. The harvest is ready to be brought home.

> Now that the harvest is gathered and you stand in the autumn of your life, your oar is no longer a driving force carrying you over the oceans of your inner and outer worlds, but a spirit of discriminating wisdom, separating moment by moment the wheat of life from the chaff, so that you may know in both wheat and chaff their meaning and their value in the pattern of the universe. (Helen Lukes, "Old Age," in Fowler and McCutcheon, page 35)

"At the Offertory," a piece from the Gaelic *Saltair*, a collection of prayers that follow the form of the Eucharist, also mixes wheat and ocean metaphors:

> Christ's is the seed.
> Christ's is the harvest.
> To the barn of Christ, may we be brought.
>
> Christ's is the sea.
> Christ's is the fish.
> In the nets of Christ may we be caught.
>
> From growth to age, from age to death,
> Your two arms, Christ, around about us.
> From death to the end, not end but re-growth,
> In the Heaven of graces may we be.

In Connemara, Ireland, at the edge of the sea, again the earth and sea, the sod and salt air mix. John O'Donohue describes the burial custom of Connemara, how the sod is carefully pulled back on three sides, the coffin inserted and the sod is

...rolled out over the grave so that it fits exactly over the opening...a "cesarean section in reverse." It is as if the womb of the earth, without being broken, is receiving back the individual who once left as a clay shape to live in separation above in the world. It is an image of homecoming, of being taken back completely again. (*Anam Cara*, page 224)

CHAPTER ELEVEN

Homecoming

E ye has not seen nor ear heard,
nor has it entered into the human heart,
  what God has prepared for those who love God.
  (1 Corinthians 2:9)

Even the most active and creative imagining cannot begin to
grasp the homecoming which our good God has in store for us.
Theologian Beth Johnson comments on the above verse from
Corinthians:

> ...[H]ow deeply a legitimate agnosticism reaches, even in
> Scripture. Eschatological [end time] events partake of the
> character of ultimate mystery. What will be will be
> surprising, coming from the overflowing wellspring of life,
> the incomprehensible mystery of God. Thus theological
> language about whatever follows death is of necessity
> indirect, like language about God, proceeding by way of
> analogy, metaphor, or symbol.... (*Friends of God and
> Prophets*, page 182)

In this chapter we will offer some symbols, metaphors and
stories to reflect upon the mystery of our homecoming. We
begin with the certitude of Saint Paul. "I am quite certain that
the One who began this good work in you will see that it is
finished" (Philippians 1:6). "It is finished," Jesus proclaims from
the cross (John 19:30). We dare to believe that by our baptism
we are the Body of Christ and so, at the last moment of our life,
whatever its circumstance, we will live/die/live with Jesus: "It
is finished."

There is anecdotal evidence from persons who have
undergone a near-death experience that the homecoming is

indeed a gentle process, filled with light and warmth. For most of us, however, there is no rehearsal for this event called dying. Even the most devout believer, like an eighty-two-year-old woman of great faith, has probably wondered, at least interiorly, "Do you ever wonder whether when you wake up there won't be anything there?"

For Reflection and Prayer

What are your thoughts and feelings about your death? And what comes after? Share these ponderings with God, with Mary, with someone dear to you who is in heaven...or out loud with someone here.

When we let ourselves approach this ultimate mystery of our one and only life we may be surprised at what bubbles up in prayer. One woman, in praying about the impending death of her sixty-two-year-old brother from lung cancer was startled by the image of her deceased parents holding her brother up to God, saying, "This is my beloved son in whom I am well pleased." The surprise in that prayer experience was the certitude that for her brother, whose life had been marked by every sort of failure, including the failure to please his parents, all was well. In fact God and our loved ones in heaven see things with a different, all-compassionate eye. As this man's lung cancer grew worse his sister asked him one day what he was thinking about his dying. He laughed and said, "I think Mum will be the first one to greet me with a fresh apple pie." His mother's apple pie was legend in that family, a symbol of love, warmth, nourishment—and as his sister replied "one of the few things on earth worth dying for!"

The morning that he was dying, he had been in a coma for several hours when his younger sister called from out of state and asked that the phone be held to his ear. His last human movement was the tiniest trace of a smile. When that sister was asked after he died what she had said to him, she replied that she didn't say anything. Instead she sang him the song that their mother always sang in the car at the beginning of vacation. That song had always been a sign that vacation was really under way! Now so was his eternal rest!

The Welcoming Committee

Our Christian faith proclaims resurrection, a transforming and making whole of all that is living in us. Death temporarily separates us—in ways that often feel brutal and final. The body shell that was our loved one, that will be ourselves one day, is recognizable yet so dramatically not the same. The breath and warmth of life have stopped. What a leap of faith to believe that this separation is only temporary, that a grand, unimaginable reunion of transformed beings lies in store for us.

Our Christian belief in the communion of saints, confessed Sunday after Sunday, is one way that we try to image the Body of Christ—all those living and dead, those we know, those we don't know. In *Friends of God and Prophets* Beth Johnson tries to plumb some of the depths of this infrequently studied mystery of our faith.

> Among these saints are also numbered some whom we knew personally. Their number increases as we get older: grandparents, mother and father, sisters and brothers, beloved spouses and life partners, children, teachers, students, patients, clients, friends and colleagues, relatives and neighbors, spiritual guides and religious leaders. Their good lives, complete with fault and failure, have reached journey's end. Gone from us, they have arrived home in unspeakable unimaginable life within the embrace of God. (page 233)

Those who have gone before us in faith cannot communicate about their experience in the ordinary ways of human communication. But by way of "memory" and "hope" we, the "saints" here on earth, do have access to this, our welcoming committee in heaven (Johnson, page 234). This is not static memory but the same kind of dynamic and effective memory that we invoke in every celebration of the Eucharist. Each one of us has a treasure trove of memory which, whenever it is evoked, is still able to give life and energy. "Saints on earth have access to the company of the saints in heaven through memory and hope. Memory is meant here in the sense of anamnesis, an effective remembering that makes something genuinely past to be present and active in the community today," Johnson explains.

And then there is the dynamic genetic memory that each of us carries. Haven't we sometimes been surprised by joy at the appearance of a beloved parent's characteristic in one of our own children, grandchildren, nieces or nephews? The mysterious strand of life that is passed from generation to generation keeps our ancestors alive in all their human glory and frailty.

O'Donohue tells a story of the multitude of ancestors, always alive in Celtic spirituality: "A priest, pestered by a friend as to where one might find the dead, finally raised his right hand and beneath it the questioner saw all the 'departed ones everywhere all around as thick as the dew on the blades of grass.' O'Donohue then comments on the story: "Often our loneliness and isolation are the result of a failure of spiritual imagination" (page 227). What we think of as empty space is, for the Celtic mind, filled with presences. The "unity in friendship that we call *anam cara* overcomes even death" (page 229). Of course, these dead friends and ancestors care even more deeply for us. They are, as the British say of their village constables, "the minders of frails."

Beth Johnson, too, calls on the Celtic tradition. In researching the history of the feast of All Saints, Beth notes that November 1 was established by the eighth century in transalpine Europe, probably an attempt to replace the Druids' feast of Samhain. "In the northern climate, the gathering of the harvest coupled with the waning of the sun and the approach of dark winter signaled the beginning of the new year on November 1. The Celts believed that the souls of those who had died during the year traveled to the other world at this time" (*Friends of God and Prophets*, page 98).

Award-winning novelist of *Charming Billy*, Alice McDermott, too, chimes in with the story of relationships continuing beyond the grave. The narrator of the novel is speaking of her parents' love, now culminating as the wife is dying of lung cancer:

...Their meeting, their courtship, their years raising children, every ordinary day they had spent together until then all became merely the running start they had taken to vault this moment. To sail, gracefully and in tandem, across the abyss.

It made it easier that they both believed in the simplest kind of afterlife—that my father could say to her, even in those last days, joking but without irony, 'You're going to get tired of hearing from me. I'll be asking you about this and that and the other thing twenty-four hours a day. Jesus, you'll be saying, here comes another prayer from Dennis.' And my mother would reply, her voice hoarse with pain, 'Jesus might advise you to take in a movie once in a while. Give your poor wife a rest. She's in heaven, after all.'...

...It was clear now that they would love each other until the last moment of her life—hadn't that been the goal from the beginning? They would love each other even beyond the days they had lived together; was there any greater triumph? (pages 52-53)

It is not only Christian or Irish belief that enriches our images of the homecoming. Some good news on the secular scene as well. In an advertisement for therapists who deal with grief was this startling statement:

Despite cultural disapproval and lack of validation by professionals, survivors find places for the dead in their ongoing lives and even in their communities. Such bonds are not denial; the deceased can provide resources for enriched functioning in the process. (*Continuing Bonds: New Understandings of Grief*)

Frequently throughout this book we have revisited in detail various memories of our lives. As we contemplate the persons who have gone before us we may be able to taste again their life and love. Many of us experience the immediacy of these, our own "saints." We call on them in trouble. We talk our problems over with them. And we are forever ambushed by surprising reminders that they are alive and well in this new transformation of being. Sometimes we "hear" their voices. This does happen, and not just during those days of intense grieving when it is normal to "see" the person we have lost. At the core of our Christian hope is the certitude that they will be with us in our passage from life through death into new life. With Jesus and Mary, they will be our "welcoming committee."

For Reflection and Prayer

Imagine the scene of your own death. On earth, who do you want there with you? In heaven? Who is standing with Jesus and Mary waiting to greet you as you cross the finish line? Talk with them. Share your fears and hopes and deepest desires about this homecoming. Listen for what they may say to you.

Rea often asks those she directs what they mean by a "happy death." Then she was surprised herself. Just two weeks before the deadline for this book, Rea underwent a powerful experience that opened her eyes to what so many of our readers have, do or will experience: a belief, a feeling, a pain that may have meant she was dying. Rea's friends and many of her acquaintances know her fear of death, especially every time she boards an airplane. She has also made it known that for her a happy death would be about three months' notice so she could say goodbye to her loved ones. She wants to die conscious and consciously.

At 1:25 in the morning of April 16, as she awoke from sleep, Rea was startled by a very sharp pain below her left breast, so sharp she couldn't move. Turning on the light was an effort. Finally after 15 minutes she decided to move, regardless of the pain. For an hour and a half she sat in a chair near the bedroom door of one of the sisters, so she could call for help if she needed it. And then she pictured her welcoming committee; she felt the joy of seeing Jesus and Mary; she felt herself consciously letting go of all her projects and deadlines and self-importance; more importantly she let go of her need to say goodbye to her friends. With a deep peace, she began to realize she was having a "happy death" in this pain, this dark silence and solitude.

Besides the images and feelings, the particular Scripture

that comforted her was a pastiche of quotations from John's Gospel: "For this I was sent into the world. For this I came: to glorify your name. Shall I say, Save me from this hour? No, it was for this hour that I came. Father, glorify your name." And one line from Job: "Naked I came into this world and naked I leave it."

As the pain subsided she fixed up the couch next to the sister's door and immediately fell asleep. When she woke in the morning it was with a freedom to live or a freedom to die, but most importantly, a freedom from fear of dying. Jesus had "delivered from the fear of death all those who for their entire life were held in slavery to that fear" (Hebrews 2:15).

Although this may seem to Rea like a rehearsal of the "real thing," an experience a number of us have had, we are probably in for a great surprise. Some of us will meet loved ones for the first time—all of those ancestors who pray for us and with us down the ages. One woman who lost her mother when she was born takes great comfort in imagining her mother coming to greet and claim her, even before Jesus meets her at the moment of death. Our faith's certitude about the presence of our loved ones in heaven can calm some of the fear of dying, so human and real.

We cannot imagine what this will be like anymore than the unborn baby can imagine all the wonders of life beyond the womb. Our faith promises this new transformed life, as different from our life here as our fully lived lives are from our fetal life within our mother. As Saint Paul says, "Now we are seeing a dim reflection in a mirror; but then we shall be seeing face to face. The knowledge that I have now is imperfect; but then I shall know as fully as I am known" (1 Corinthians 13:12). How do we even begin to think about that reality?

For Reflection and Prayer

Sit quietly with the words of Saint Paul. What bubbles up for you? What thoughts, images, feelings, people?

God's Welcome

What about God's welcome? Do we have any hint of what that might be like? Jesus gives us an idea in his story of the "prodigal son." "While he was still a long way off, his father saw him and was moved with pity. He ran to the boy, clasped him in his arms and kissed him tenderly" (Luke 15:20). Sometimes, because of our real or imagined sins, we live in fear of the judgment of God. But we need to know that down all the labyrinthine ways of each of our lives God has been watching for us, waiting for our homecoming, waiting to welcome us tenderly and with infinite mercy. Who can imagine the depths of God's compassion? It doesn't matter where or how we may have squandered the gifts of our life. God's mercy is so much greater than our capacity for sin. "Nothing can come between us and the love of Christ.... neither death nor life...nothing still to come, not any power, or heights or depths...can come between us and the love of God..." (Romans 8:38-39). Mother Teresa of Calcutta put it this way: "There is no need to fear death because death is nothing more than going home to God. For me, that is the greatest development of a human life: to die in peace with God."

We forget that God is the good farmer. "To cite the agricultural metaphor used in 1 Corinthians, the risen Christ can be seen as the first of the fruits to ripen and be plucked, but all the beloved dead will make up the rest of the harvest" (Johnson, page 65). Our good God once and for all transforms the wheat of our lives into the risen body of Christ.

Perhaps our best image of resurrection from the dead also comes from Paul's First Letter to the Corinthians. Recent theology is beginning to assume that, like Jesus and Mary, we will receive our risen bodies immediately after death, our persons having outgrown these shells, like the soft-shell crab of Maryland. Again, Paul uses the agricultural image:

> Some will ask: How are the dead raised? With what kind of body do they come? ...What you sow, you do not sow the body that is to be, but a bare seed, perhaps of wheat or of some other grain. So it is with the resurrection of the

dead. What is sown is perishable, what is raised is imperishable. It is sown in dishonor, it is raised in glory. It is sown in weakness, it is raised in power. It is sown a physical body, it is raised a spiritual body. If there is a physical body, there is also a spiritual body.
(1 Corinthians 15)

The seed, our human body, contains all its growth within it. When God plants it, it is dark and hard and small. When it pushes through the earth it is green and flexible and supportive of life. It is transformed; it is from the seed, but it no longer resembles the seed. It is reborn. It is new.

Nothing Is Lost

In the sixth chapter of John's Gospel we hear Jesus promise that he is the "bread of life." Many times during our lifetime on earth we have been nourished by this bread in the Eucharist. Our homecoming is the final affirmation of Jesus' promise: "Who comes to me will never be hungry. Who believes in me will never thirst" (John 6:25).

During the course of this book we have reverently recalled and remembered the grains of wheat that have been sown and grown and harvested in our own lives. In this final homecoming we believe they (we) are transformed eternally into the Bread that is the Body of Christ, risen, glorified, and finally triumphant over all the evil that has ever been. In this same profound chapter of John's Gospel we listen to Jesus promise: "...the will of the One who sent me is that I should lose nothing of all that God has given to me, and that I should raise it up on the last day" (John 6:39-40).

Nothing is lost. Not a tear, not a good work, not a one of our frail and flawed ways of loving will ever be lost—amazing grace. And so we sing:

When we've been there ten thousand years
bright shining as the sun
We've no less days to sing God's praise
than when we first begun.

We can sing with the psalmist:

> Our life is a mere seventy years,
> eighty for those in good health,
> All it gives us is toil and distress;
> Then the thread breaks and we are gone....
> Teach us to make use of our days
> and bring wisdom to our hearts.
>
> Shine your love on us each dawn, and gladden all
>   our days.
> Balance our past sorrows with present joys
> Let your servants, young and old, see the splendor
>   of your work.
> Let your loveliness shine on us.... (Psalm 90)

We can sing with Simeon: "Lord, now may your servant die in peace, for you kept your promise. With my own eyes I can see the salvation you prepared for all peoples, a light of revelation to the Gentiles and glory of your people Israel" (Luke 2: 29-32).

We can sing with generations of African Americans:

> Precious Lord take my hand, lead me on, let me stand.
>   I am tired, I am weak, I am worn—
> Through the storm, through the night, lead me on to
>   the light.
> Take my hand, precious Lord, lead me home.
>
> When my way grows drear, precious Lord, linger near.
> When my life is almost gone—
> Hear my cry, hear my call, hold my hand lest I fall.
> Take my hand, precious Lord, lead me home.
>
> When the darkness appears and the night draws near,
>   and the day is past and gone—
> At the river I stand, guide my feet, hold my hand.
> Take my hand, precious Lord, lead me home.

We can sing with the disciples on the road to Emmaus: "Stay with us, Lord. It is getting toward evening" (Luke 24:29).

We can sing with Ignatius of Loyola:

> Take, O Lord, and receive all my liberty, my memory, my
> understanding, and my entire will, all that I have and

possess. You have given all to me. To you, Lord, I return it. All is yours. Dispose of it according to your will. Give me your love and your grace, for this is enough for me.

Yet we choose to conclude this song that will never end with our Mother Mary, our pioneer in aging, in growing in wisdom, age and grace, always becoming more fully human and more fully alive: "Let it be done unto me according to your word" (Luke 1:38).

BIBLIOGRAPHY

Albom, Mitch. *Tuesdays with Morrie*. New York: Doubleday, 1998.

Becker, Ernest. *The Denial of Death*. New York: Free Press, 1973.

Bianchi, Eugene. *On Growing Older*. New York: Crossroad, 1985.

Billig, Nathan. *Growing Older and Wiser: Coping with Expectations, Challenges, and Change in the Later Years*. New York: Lexington Books of Macmillan, Inc., 1993.

_____. *To Be Old and Sad: Understanding Depression in the Elderly*. Lexington, Mass.: Lexington Books, 1987.

Bird, Caroline. *Lives of Our Own: Secrets of Salty Old Women*. New York: Houghton Mifflin, 1995.

Borsyenko, Joan. *A Woman's Book of Life: The Biology, Psychology, and Spirituality of the Feminine Life Cycle*. New York: Random House, 1996.

Burghardt, Walter, S.J. *Seasons That Laugh or Weep: Musings on the Human Journey*. New York: Paulist, 1983.

Cahill, Dorothy Anne, C.S.C. "Tempus," in *Weavings*, vol. xiv, no. 1, Jan/Feb, 1999, page 33.

Callahan, Rachel, C.S.C., and Rea McDonnell, S.S.N.D. *God Is Close to the Brokenhearted: Good News for Those Who Are Depressed*. Cincinnati: St. Anthony Messenger Press, 1997.

_____. *Hope for Healing: Good News for Adult Children of Alcoholics*. Dubuque, Iowa: Islewest, 1998.

_____ *Welcome Home, Healing Your Broken Heart* (audiotape). Cincinnati: St. Anthony Messenger Press, 1996.

_____ *Wholing the Heart: Good News for Those Who Grew Up in Troubled Families*. Dubuque, Iowa: Islewest, 1998.

Cameron, Julia. *The Artist's Way: A Spiritual Path to Higher Creativity*. New York: A Jeremy P. Tarcher/Putnam Book, G.P. Putnam's Sons, 1992.

Catechism of the Catholic Church. Libreria Editrice Vaticana. Mahwah, N.J.: Paulist Press, 1994.

Coles, Robert. *Old and on Their Own.* New York: W.W. Norton & Company, Inc., 1998.

Duke, Horace. *Where Is God When Bad Things Happen?* St. Meinrad, Ind.: St. Meinrad Press, 1995.

Dychtwald, Ken, and Joe Flower. *Age Wave: The Challenges and Opportunities of An Aging America.* Los Angeles: Jeremy P. Tarcher, Inc., 1989.

Erikson, Erik. *The Life Cycle Completed.* New York: W.W. Norton & Company, Inc., 1982.

Ferder, Fran, F.S.P.A. *Words Made Flesh.* Notre Dame, Ind.: Ave Maria Press, 1986.

Finch, Ann, ed. *Journey to the Light: Spirituality as We Mature.* New York: New York City Press, 1993.

Fischer, Kathleen. *Autumn Gospel.* Mahwah, N.J.: Paulist Press, 1995.

_____. *Winter Grace.* Mahwah, N.J.: Paulist Press, 1985.

Fowler, Margaret, and Priscilla McCutcheon, eds. *Songs of Experience: An Anthology of Literature on Growing Old.* New York: Ballantine Books, 1991.

Friedan, Betty. *The Fountain of Age.* New York: Simon and Schuster, 1993.

Hall, Douglas John. *God and Human Suffering.* Minneapolis: Augsburg, 1986.

Harris, Maria. *Proclaim Jubilee: A Spirituality for the Twenty-First Century.* Louisville, Ky.: Westminster-John Knox Press, 1996.

Hopkins, Gerard Manley, S.J. *The Poems of Gerard Manley Hopkins,* fourth edition, eds. W. H. Gardner and N. H. MacKenzie. London: Oxford University Press, 1967.

Houselander, Caryll. *The Reed of God*. Allen, Texas: Christian Classics, 1944.

Howard, Julie. "You Are There" (song lyrics). Collegeville, Minn.: Order of St. Benedict.

Ingram, Kristen Johnson. "The Sacrament of Time," *Weavings*, vol. xiv, no. 1, Jan/Feb, 1999, pages 26-32.

Johnson, Elizabeth. *Friends of God and Prophets*. New York: Continuum, 1998.

Klass, Dennis, Phyllis Silverman, and Steven Nickman, eds. *Continuing Bonds: New Understandings of Grief*. Levittown, Penn.: Taylor and Francis, 1996.

Kushner, Harold S. *How Good Do We Have to Be? A New Understanding of Guilt and Forgiveness*. Boston: Little, Brown and Company, 1996.

Levine, Stephen. *Healing Into Life and Death*. New York: Doubleday (Anchor Books), 1987.

Lindgren, Maggy, S.N.D. "Grace," unpublished poem, February 6, 1998.

Linn, Dennis and Matthew, S.J. *Healing Life's Hurts: Healing Memories Through the Five Stages of Forgiveness*. New York: Paulist Press, 1978.

Long, William. "Psychotherapy with Older Adults," seminar sponsored by American Healthcare Institute, Baltimore, January 11, 1999.

Lynch, William F., S.J. *Images of Hope: Imagination as Healer of the Hopeless*. Baltimore: Helicon Press, 1965.

Lyon, K. Brynolf. *Toward A Practical Theology of Aging*. Philadelphia: Fortress, 1985.

Maitland, David J. *Aging as Countercultural: A Vocation for the Later Years*. New York: Pilgrim Press, 1981.

Manning, Martha. *Undercurrents: A Therapist's Reckoning With Depression.* San Francisco: HarperSanFrancisco, 1994.

Martz, Sandra Haldeman, ed. *If I had my life to live over, I would pick more daisies.* Watsonville, Calif.: Papier-Mache Press, 1992.

McDermott, Alice. *Charming Billy.* New York: Farrar, Straus and Giroux, 1998.

McDonnell, Rea, S.S.N.D. *When God Comes Close.* Boston: Daughters of St. Paul, 1994.

Missinine, Leo E., M. Afr. *Reflections on Aging: A Spiritual Guide.* Liguori, Mo.: Liguori Press, 1990.

O'Donohue, John. *Anam Cara: A Book of Celtic Wisdom.* New York: HarperCollins, 1997.

O'Fiannachta, Padraig. *Saltair*, trans. Desmond Forrestal. Dublin: Columba Press, 1988.

Palmer, Charlotte. *Gifts of Age.* San Francisco: Chronicle Books, 1985.

Puls, Joan, O.S.F. *A Spirituality of Compassion.* Mystic, Conn.: Twenty-Third Publications, 1988.

Raub, John Jacob, O.S.C.O. *Who Told You That You Were Naked? Freedom from Judgment, Guilt, and Fear of Punishment.* New York: Crossroad, 1995.

Richard, Lucien, O.M.I. *What Are They Saying About the Theology of Suffering?* Mahwah, N.J.: Paulist Press, 1992.

Rowe, John W. and Robert L. Kahn. *Successful Aging.* New York: Pantheon Books, 1998.

Sarton, May. *After the Stroke: A Journal.* New York: W. W. Norton & Company, Inc., 1988.

_____. *At Eighty-Two: A Journal.* New York: W. W. Norton & Company, Inc., 1996.

_____. *The House by the Sea*. New York: W. W. Norton & Company, Inc., 1981.

Schachter-Shalomi, Zalman, and Ronald S. Miller. *Age-ing to Sage-ing*. New York: Warner Books, 1995.

Smith, Harold Ivan. *On Grieving the Death of a Father*. Minneapolis: Augsburg, 1994.

Sullivan, Paula. *The Mystery of My Story: Autobiographical Writing for Personal and Spiritual Development*. Mahwah, N.J.: Paulist Press, 1991.

Teilhard de Chardin, Pierre, S.J. *The Divine Milieu*. New York: Harper & Brothers, 1957.

Thurston, Bonnie Bowman. *The Widows: A Women's Ministry in the Early Church*. Minneapolis: Fortress Press, 1989.

Valentine, Mary Hester, S.S.N.D. *Aging in the Lord*. New York: Paulist, 1994.

Viorst, Judith. *Necessary Losses: The Loves, Illusions, Dependencies and Impossible Expectations That We All Have to Give Up in Order to Grow*. New York: Simon and Schuster, 1986.

Wiederkehr, Macrina, O.S.B. *Gold in Your Memories: Sacred Moments, Glimpses of God*. Notre Dame, Ind.: Ave Maria Press, 1998.

Wright, Wendy. "Resting Reaping Times," *Weavings*, vol. xiv, no. 1, Jan/Feb, 1999, pages 6-14.